MW01059529

BIGFOOT IN MAINE

MICHELLE Y. SOULIERE

Introduction by Loren Coleman, Founder & Director of the
International Cryptozoology Museum, Portland, Maine

Happy hunting!

THE
History
PRESS

Published by The History Press
Charleston, SC
www.historypress.com

Copyright © 2021 by Michelle Souliere
All rights reserved

Cover: "He's Over There!" *Illustration by Michelle Y. Souliere. Back*: Signs of wear and tear in Maine's wildlife sanctuaries. *Photo by Michelle Y. Souliere.*

First published 2021

Manufactured in the United States

ISBN 9781467147484

Library of Congress Control Number: 2021931127

Notice: The information in this book is true and complete to the best of our knowledge. It is offered without guarantee on the part of the author or The History Press. The author and The History Press disclaim all liability in connection with the use of this book.

Dedicated to all those who love the State of Maine in all its weird glory.

CONTENTS

DISCLAIMER: WATCH YOUR STEP, PLEASE!

Bigfoot in Maine is not intended as a guide to trespassing. Unfortunately, as fellow authors have found, it is impossible to control people who choose to break the law, vandalize or destroy locations discussed in print and online. The Maine areas mentioned herein are presented in connection with local legends and oral history encountered in my research. This book is intended to be read with the knowledge that most of the places mentioned are or might become private property or are otherwise legally off limits, and as such cannot be visited without permission, if at all.

This disclaimer serves the purpose of clearly stating that *trespassing is illegal*. Those who disregard this warning can, and often will, be arrested and charged accordingly. Trips to any of the locations featured in this book are undertaken as a personal choice of the reader and not at the instigation of the author. Michelle Souliere and the book *Bigfoot in Maine* do not support trespassing, law breaking or acts of vandalism of any kind.

Please keep in mind best practices if visiting the Maine wilderness and follow the very important basic principles of leave no trace:

1. Plan ahead and prepare.
2. Travel and camp on durable surfaces.
3. Minimize campfire impacts (be careful with fire).
4. Be considerate of other visitors.
5. Leave what you find.
6. Dispose of waste properly.
7. Respect wildlife.

DISCLAIMER: WATCH YOUR STEP, PLEASE!

As I learned when researching this book, it is important when planning a hike to stay aware of hunting season dates and vital to wear a blaze orange cap and/or clothing when outdoors at those times. You can check Maine hunting season dates here:

https://www.maine.gov/ifw/hunting-trapping/hunting-laws /season-dates-bag-limits.html

PREFACE

When I started writing this book over ten years ago, it was manifestly different in my mind than what you hold in your hands now.

Two major events shaped these changes: first, Loren Coleman bowed out as cowriter due to circumstances beyond his control, which required me to throw my net wider (and to stand on my own two feet), and second, Daniel Green wrote a book about Bigfoot in Maine that duplicated a large amount of the historical source material I dug up to give readers as a collective resource, thereby nullifying a large part of my original goal for this book.

While this was frustrating, it was an opportunity to test my mettle. What should I do with this beast of a book? I decided to do what had yet to be done—look at the patterns and fascinating ins and outs of Maine's history with Bigfoot and, even more importantly, explore its effect on the people of Maine.

I interviewed people about their encounters and dug for hours through historic and digital archives to thread together stories buried for decades or more. Many incidents seemed isolated, but others spawned a contagion of rumored sightings. Some reflected Bigfoot-related trends in the world at large, while others were as independent as any Mainer.

Eyewitnesses told me varied tales, but all were permanently affected by what they encountered, whether it terrified or just baffled them. Many were haunted by a certain puzzlement. What was this thing they had seen or heard? What did it mean to them, and what did it mean in the greater scheme of things? Most went on with their lives, knowing they would never have a good explanation for their encounter, and until recently, most kept their mouths shut about it.

Maine Bigfoot experiences only come out in small company, where it's safe to talk and everyone present knows their local history. There are, I am sure, countless stories I have not heard for just that reason. Why bother to tell your tale to some woman who lives way down in Portland? She's never spent days on end up in the woods where you are.

I talked to a lot of people and heard about some incredibly intriguing events. I also floundered—sometimes when you talk to people, the conversation starts out well, but then a switch gets flipped as they realize they locked this experience away in their head for a reason, and now you are the enemy because you have made them remember it. All the associated dredged-up turmoil swamps them and causes them to lash out at you. There were setbacks.

There were also moments when the realization of what I could do with this book, and the untold stories that I was going to be able to bring forward to contribute to Maine's oral history, made my heart sing and set my brain on fire. I'm still surprised I heard as many accounts as I did, taking chances I might be stopped cold by someone's unwillingness to share. I owe a debt of gratitude to everyone who took me at my word and shared their knowledge with me.

Many of the older stories I researched will never be fully known, the players in those dramas long dead. But the encounters I am able to tell you here will now live on and be joined by the next generation of Maine encounters. The bravery of those who came forward to share their experiences in case it might help someone else is something I will never forget.

I hope that you, dear reader, enjoy what is collected here for you and that it feeds your curiosity. I hope you find these accounts as fascinating as I have and that this book brings forth more surprising histories from the darkest corners of the Maine woods, where they otherwise would have moldered, consumed by the natural process of time and decay into the very material of the forest floor itself, whispered only on the wind.

Enjoy!

ACKNOWLEDGEMENTS

As this project spanned more than a decade, understandably, there are a lot of people to thank. Some remain anonymous, and some memories might have blurred in the intervening years. If you do not see your name here, it is not due to lack of gratitude but to the fallible organ known as the human brain, for which I apologize wholeheartedly.

First and foremost, I must thank both Loren and Jenny Coleman for years of support and friendship. This book wouldn't exist without Loren. Even when things looked bleakest, he would exhort me, "Don't wait to finish the book! Write it now!" Jenny's strength, compassion and sense of humor in the face of every obstacle continues to be an inspiration.

The other people without whom this book would not exist are the eyewitnesses who trusted me enough to talk to me. This is your book—you are the heart and soul of it. Without your experiences, I wouldn't be writing this. Thank you for sharing, thank you for your time answering my many questions and thank you on behalf of the silent eyewitnesses who might be helped by reading your accounts. Some of you have withstood years of ridicule and stigma because of something you had no control over. But in the end, you know what you experienced, and nothing can change that. I did my best to accurately tell your narratives. Any mistakes in interpreting the course of events are my own—hopefully they are few and far between.

Speaking of eyewitnesses, I am indebted to fellow author and Strange Maine-iac Nomar Slevik for referring a number of witnesses to me. I hope I can continue to do the same for you, my friend.

In the scholarly realm, support and assistance was given by a wide range of excellent and knowledgeable people. Early on, Chuck Flood helped in the hunt for historic articles. Herb Adams kept his eye peeled for newspaper articles and cheered me on. Author Ken Buckley revisited his news reporting days on my behalf and helped me find articles from decades ago. Across the country, Rex Valentine, dowser and cattleman, dove into his memories of a bygone day to dig up old ghosts for me and, in the process, became a new friend. Dr. Michael Swords, guardian of Ivan Sanderson's papers and the archives of the Society for the Investigation of the Unknown, aided me with materials from his vast experience and friendly words. Doug Skinner, friend and trustee of John. A. Keel, likewise, pored through files in search of loose ends.

The experts in the black bear biology field who took the time to answer my questions (probably while scratching their heads over them) have my gratitude, as well, especially Dr. Roy Hugie and Dr. Craig McLaughlin. Maine state biologists Jennifer Vashon and Randy Cross took time out from their black bear fieldwork to weigh in where they could, as well.

Many a pleasant day was spent on field trips with friends who were willing to drive all over creation and wade through almost anything in my company. Field expeditions have been my absolute favorite part of this, and I hope this tradition of outdoor escapades continues for many years. My stalwart companions in these adventures include registered Maine guide Dustin Howe, who took a chance on teaching me outdoors(wo)manship in all seasons and how to navigate with map and compass in the woods; adventuress extraordinaire Salli Wason, who piloted me through the wild and untamed backroads all over Maine; the indefatigable Dave T.; and my ever-supportive husband, Tristan, who helped me keep a sense of humor and perspective throughout the years of this work.

Occasionally, I was unable to travel to pinpoint locations or revisit sites for documentation. In a testament to our longstanding friendship and mutual love of weird adventure, filmmaker Christian Matzke helped me more than once in these endeavors, providing me with amazing assistance when all I could do was cross my fingers and hope.

Thanks also goes out to friend and filmmaker Andy Davis, who knows Maine's weirdness like the back of his hand and loves it just as much as I do. To Andy and Rick Dalton and all those who talked to me about their Bigfoot-related creative endeavors in the early stages of this book, know that while your stories did not wind up in the final version of the book, I will be printing them in articles on the *Strange Maine* blog and in the *Strange Maine Gazette*, so they will still be heard.

A special shoutout must also go to the eyewitnesses who took a large part of their day to familiarize me with the location of their sightings and the surrounding region, which was extraordinarily helpful and very generous, considering I was a total stranger to them before our outings. I am happy to now have you as my friends.

When researching at a distance, I was gratified and relieved to encounter some extremely helpful and diligent library staff in Maine and elsewhere. Never underestimate your local library!

The now-defunct Maine Folklife Archives in Orono (subsumed into UMaine's Fogler Library) was made imminently more accessible by Katrina Wynn, who assisted me repeatedly on my Strange Maine projects over the years, providing invaluable resources and aid.

Abraham Schechter persists in making the Portland Room at the Portland Public Library a growing resource for historians everywhere—our city's hidden gem.

Lynne Holland, a volunteer at Brunswick's Curtis Memorial Library, went above and beyond many times to help me pull together widely flung threads of historical elements buried in the Brunswick/Durham area archives.

Elizabeth Stevens, hard at work in the Local History/Special Collections at Bangor Public Library, got roped into helping me find all sorts of articles after an introduction from Ken Buckley, and provided me with a few real "eureka!" moments that are rare in this type of research.

Jamie Kingman-Rice, now director of collections and research at Maine Historical Society's Library, has for many years been a stalwart and friendly ally in the search for obscure Maine historical resources and documents.

Cheri Bellavance and Kent Nelson at the Maine Forest Service did their best to answer questions about historic Maine fires, even when state records faltered.

Lastly, many states away, Eric S. Crow, reference assistant at Wisconsin Historical Society, very cooperatively unearthed scans of early historical letters referring to Daniel Boone, which can be found nowhere else, and made them available to me. While the material did not go into this book, since it turned out to be only peripherally related, I will be writing a separate article about what I found.

INTRODUCTION

Whether it be snowing outside or a ninety-degree day, how can I not but pen a love letter to Maine?

Maine is beautiful: 95 percent of the landscape is covered with trees, lakes, rivers and creeks; pitcher plants in the bogs; evergreen trees year-round; birds from the tropics in the summer and hardy seasoned chickadees, snowy owls and blue jays in the winter.

The border along the Atlantic Ocean is framed in rocky coasts and sandy beaches. The skies are filled with clean, fresh air, in which the pesky gnats we call no-see-'ems are considered not a menace but evidence that the streams they breed in are unpolluted. If Bigfoot wished to pick a state to raise its family and live for generations on generations for hundreds of years, they could not have chosen a better, more inviting, often isolated location.

Other animals have done so too. Megafauna from the last Ice Age, including moose and black bear, have been here for tens of thousands of years. Hints of mountain lion and wolf populations live among the deer, coyote, bobcat, lynx, badger, woodchuck, wolverine and beaver who inhabit Maine's forests.

In an area the size of all the rest of New England combined, the people and its wild animals have plenty of room to stretch their legs. Only one million people dot the vast land that is Maine. This results in miles on miles of undisturbed reaches of woods.

We all think we know what Maine is, but of course Maine lives as more than a place on the map. It lives in history. It is a state of mind. It dwells in a past that is broader than the location we know today as Maine.

The District of Maine

"What is Maine?" would seem to be a relatively easy question to answer, but it is not. And indeed, the answer in time and space has some bearing on Maine's cryptozoology, which is the study of the undiscovered, unknown and hidden creatures, monsters and possible new species of the Pine Tree State.

Today, Maine exists in what is termed the New England region of the northern United States of America. Maine was once itself a crypto-creature in the Commonwealth of Massachusetts. Massachusetts, which today is the seventh-smallest state in the United States. But Massachusetts used to be huge. Today, Massachusetts is the most populous New England state and the third most densely populated state in the United States. But it once contained what would become one of the least populated states.

For two hundred years, Maine has been a state. Before that, the territory was a forgotten wild corner of upper Massachusetts, technically the District of Maine. In the district, adventurers went hunting, fishing, hiking and camping, and four groups of Native Americans and First Peoples from indigenous America lived and traveled back and forth between our northern neighbor, Canada, and the United States of America, often ignored and neglected.

The prehistoric and historical background of the state has a direct relationship to names, stories and records of its monsters. Tribes of the Algonquian language family, such as the Wampanoag, Narragansett, Nipmuc, Pocomtuc, Mahican and Massachusett, originally inhabited Massachusetts.

Meanwhile, Maine was home to several recognized tribes. In the 1700s, the Micmac, Maliseet, Passamaquoddy, Abenaki and Penobscot people joined together in an alliance known as the Wabanaki Confederacy. Their descendants still live here.

But few today realize that from the time the Massachusetts Bay Colony was established in 1630 until 1820, all of what today is Maine was part of Massachusetts. Maine voted to secede and on March 15, 1820, was admitted to the union as the twenty-third state under the Missouri Compromise.

During the 190 years between 1630 and 1820, any Maine sightings of cryptids, creatures and monsters would have been historically recorded, most properly, as accounts from Massachusetts. Therefore, pre-1820 accounts might be confusing.

THE AROOSTOOK TRIANGLE

As you take this journey with investigator Michelle Souliere, you will note that as a Maine resident, she has a keen eye for discoveries. For example, during the time she was working on this book, she began to notice hints of an enigmatic area in the state, called a "triangle" or "window area" by those who study such things, in the upper tier of Maine.

The territory of this narrow wedge centered on a strong system of waterways angling south-southwest from Presque Isle.* Souliere learned about it as she ran across more and more stories. Souliere presented on this mysterious area at the International Cryptozoology Conference of 2018 as a kind of Bermuda Triangle in Maine.

"Of the stories I've heard, a number of them all take place in this little triangle in the northeast quadrant. Ten miles at its base and twenty-five miles tip-to-tip in this isolated area around US Route 1," Michelle Souliere said in her lecture.

Souliere related stories about a series of mysterious woodland encounters—wood knocks, snapping trees, large rocks being thrown and unidentifiable roars that left those who experienced them forever changed.

These all linked to Bigfoot characteristics, but Souliere was carefully correct to point to the collective unexplainable nature of these pieces of evidence. There is no telling what is making all of these signs, but it is intriguing that Souliere discovered a concentration of such reports in one specific remote area.

This area, which was locally nameless, I have coined the Aroostook Triangle, for that is where it is located, near Presque Isle.

This triangle, like Aroostook County itself, is sparely populated. Formed in 1839, Aroostook County has the largest area of any county in New

_____

* Presque Isle is the commercial center and largest city in Aroostook County, Maine. Presque Isle is also the headquarters of the Aroostook Band of Micmac, a federally recognized tribe with, at last estimate, a population of 960. Like their kin in Canada, the Micmac in Maine would rather be termed Mi'kmaq, the spelling Micmac being "colonially tainted." *Lnu* (the adjectival and singular noun, previously spelled *L'nu*; plural *Lnúk, Lnu'k, Lnu'g* or *Lnùg*) is the term the Mi'kmaq use for themselves, their autonym, meaning "human being" or "the people."

The Mi'kmaq or Mi'gmaq (also Micmac, Lnu, Mi'kmaw or Mi'gmaw) are a First Nations people indigenous to Canada's Atlantic Provinces and the Gaspé Peninsula of Quebec, as well as the northeastern region of Maine. They call their national territory Mi'kma'ki (or Mi'gmagi). The nation has a population of about 170,000 (including 18,044 members in the recently formed Qalipu First Nation in Newfoundland), of whom nearly 11,000 speak Mi'kmaq, an Eastern Algonquian language. Once written in Mi'kmaq hieroglyphic writing, it is now written using letters of the Latin alphabet.

England, and Maine residents often simply call it the County. Britannica says its name is derived from a Mi'kmaq word meaning "clear" or "beautiful water." Some other dictionaries say the meaning is unknown, which would fit well with the stories of this triangle.

Maine Is Bigfoot Country

Strange hairy creatures, upright, human-like in shape and unclassified in zoology and anthropology, have been given the popular English name of Sasquatch and Bigfoot in North America. Due to the links to the Algonquian (or Algonkian) language groupings created by anthropologists and linguists, the indigenous peoples in Maine would more often than not call these forest giants by the Anglicized form, Windigo.[*]

Both of the monikers *Bigfoot* and *Sasquatch*, unlike what most people think, did not come from the Native peoples of the land but were created by journalists.

Sasquatch was a term coined by writer J.W. Burns, a former schoolteacher on the British Columbian Chehalis First Peoples reservation. His article "Introducing British Columbia's Hairy Giants," for the Canadian news publication *Maclean's Magazine*, was the first to widely share the word *Sasquatch*. J.W. Burns's creation of the word gave the bipedal hairy beasts an Indian-sounding name, which immediately leapt into modern consciousness. Later research revealed that Native Canadians had been using words for the forest giants including *sokqueatl*, *soss-q'tal* and especially the Chehalis Halkemeylem dialect term *sesquac* for decades. Burns probably constructed the new word *Sasquatch* from his transliteration of those terms.

The popular Animal Planet program *Finding Bigfoot* has taken a variation on Sasquatch, *Squatch*, and made it into a famous expression. Something being *Squatchy* is all the rage as this book goes to print.

The more familiar word for these creatures, however, is not Sasquatch, but Bigfoot. In 1958, encounters with the huge hairy creatures' tracks occurred at a road construction site at Bluff Creek, California. The roadcrew and

---

[*] These eastern North American Bigfoot were, therefore, referred to as Wiindigoo (the source of the English word, from the Ojibwe language), Wendigo, Weendigo, Windego, Wiindgoo, Windgo, Weendigo, Wiindigoo, Windago, Windiga, Wendego, Windagoo, Widjigo, Wiijigoo, Wijigo, Weejigo, Wìdjigò (in the Algonquin language), Wintigo, Wentigo, Wehndigo, Wentiko, Windgoe, Wintsigo and wīhtikōw (in the Cree language); the Proto-Algonquian term was Wintekowa.

their wives called the creature by the name Bigfoot. A letter from one of the women to a local newspaper editor began a chain reaction that remains alive today. Andrew Genzoli, a columnist and editor at the *Humboldt Times*, published the first formal use of the word on October 5, 1958, in a front-page story. The photograph of Jerry Crew, a bulldozer operator on the road-building crew, holding an enormous plaster cast of a footprint resulted in the new name being flashed around the world.

Today, Bigfoot is the name most frequently in use. Bigfoot, as current accounts and history show, are seen in the wildest parts of Maine, as you will soon discover in this remarkable historical and current documentation by archivist and author Michelle Souliere. Join her as she explores the wonderful swampy, mountainous and wooded areas of Maine.

Loren Coleman,
founder and director of the
International Cryptozoology Museum
Portland, Maine, July 31, 2019

Part I

❯❯❯❯❮❮❮❮

LAYING THE GROUNDWORK

1

THE HYPOTHESIS

Criteria for Habitation

Why Maine? Does Maine allow for such a possibility? For decades, the public has been aware of Bigfoot sightings from the Pacific Northwest, but many other regions harbor their own Bigfoot reports, rumors and folklore. Maine is no less likely to be home to these hairy cryptids, although many folks will confess this never occurred to them.

Certain qualities of Maine easily lend themselves to the possibility of a large mammal existing here side by side with existing populations. Going down a checklist of survival needs, this potential becomes quite clear.

Climate: While our winters are considered by some to be brutal, they are still livable, given access to adaptive shelters and dietary resources. Many mammals, large and small, spend winter in Maine without heading south.

Water sources: Maine is strung with networks of waterways that sprawl across the state in an embarrassment of riches. Inspect any page in your Maine atlas, and you will be astonished by the blue maze created by freshwater systems threaded throughout the state.

Landscape: Maine is vast and retains a startling amount of wilderness, even adjacent to heavily populated areas. The state is packed with a ridge-filled glacier-dug landscape, covered with forests and lakes and peppered with glacial erratics left behind in surprising places.

Concealment and travel-through: The state is blanketed with tree and brush cover. Most of Maine's forest is connected or continuous with other forested areas. Even more telling, a 1999 Maine black bear study estimated the area of Maine's viable bear habitat at 26,973 square miles. That same report points out that tree cover is paramount to bear habitat: "Bears do not persist in open grasslands or open agricultural areas without tree cover."[1]

If any of you have spent time in Maine's woods trying to spot animals, birds or a lost friend, you know how much the tree cover blurs outlines. Even at the low height and density of saplings and shrubbery, or when branches are bare in winter, the tree cover breaks up the outlines of other living things around you, so you won't even know they're there, even when large in size.

Fitting around existing human settlements: Maine's densest human populations cluster in the southern half of the state, along its coast and in the east, following the Interstate-95/US Route 1 corridor north to the Canadian border.

As of the U.S. Census in 2000, almost half of Maine remained classified as unorganized territories. When compared to other states, Maine has the third-largest area of this type. In real terms, this means Maine territories that are not part of an organized municipality total an area of 14,052 square miles. That's 45.5 percent of Maine's land area.[2] Unsurprisingly, Maine ranks at thirty-eight in population density in the United States.[3]

Food Sources: Maine is home to a vibrant array of hardy wild animal and plant populations. Again, one only has to look at the native black bear population to see that the ability of the Maine landscape to maintain daily necessities for a large mammal is not only possible but also already exists as a fact in practice.

In the decades since the Maine Department of Inland Fisheries and Wildlife began its work to understand, protect and regulate the local black bear population, it has reversed a dangerous decline in black bear numbers. Today, the Maine black bear has rebounded to the healthy population numbers hoped for when the program began, with regular ongoing bear hunting in place to carefully regulate the population.[4]

What can we learn from the known large mammals of Maine? First, we can applaud the hard work Maine biologists have done. They labored for decades, collecting and studying data in tremendous detail, much of it

Fishing in the Androscoggin River. *Illustration by Michelle Y. Souliere.*

gathered in the face of great difficulty in the field. Because of their work, we can make some observations and project some loose hypotheses based on existing knowledge.

We can say it is likely that if a Bigfoot-like creature was in Maine, it would have little in the way of alpha-predator competition, being (by all accounts) as big or bigger than Maine's known native predators. Besides human beings, this includes large animals such as bears and cougars and progressively smaller predators, such as bobcats, lynx, wolves, coyotes, fishers and foxes. Bears are a serviceable analogue for our mystery creature, with an average male black bear running between 250 and 600 pounds.[5]

We can also hypothesize that the creature would be an opportunistic eater, or omnivore, much like a black bear. That means it would make use of available plant growth and harvests, as well as meat from local wildlife.

But let's start with the veggies and move onto the protein afterward. In spring, black bears devour early grasses, clover and the buds of hardwood trees. In the summer, bears add fruits and berries to their diet as they become available. In the fall, as crops ripen, a bear's diet includes protein from beechnuts, acorns and hazelnuts in preparation for hibernation.[6]

Throughout the year, black bears include protein in their diet by eating insects such as ants and bees, including both adult and larval forms. Bears will eat other mammals, as well as birds and fish. In late spring, often at their hungriest with post-hibernation blues, they have been known to hunt and eat young deer and moose. Bears will consume carrion.

Bears roam their territories as the seasons change, and food sources shift with them. They follow the food with a remarkable recall for when and where they encountered food sources in previous years. This also seems like a reasonable attribute for our creature.

All of the ingredients and habits mentioned here could make sense as a framework for the diet of the creature we are wondering about.

I have talked to people who have found traces indicating these mystery hominids kill and eat wildfowl, and I have talked to others who are convinced they eat deer and other smaller wild and domestic mammals. I have talked to eyewitnesses who have seen them fishing with their hands in rivers and lakes and eating fish, freshwater clams and algae from ponds.

Many sightings of our mystery creature occur in areas where there are extensive native berry patches and other crops, both wild and cultivated by local farmers.

With all these things in mind, it seems a reasonable possibility that Maine could support an additional population, small in number, of reticent and omnivorous large mammals.

The Patterns: What do we really know? I can only base my own statements on what I have heard from the people I have interviewed. And while not all of them have had a visual encounter, many of them have, some with prolonged contact and even interaction. Throughout my interviews, some patterns have emerged. For purposes of discussion, I've put together a list of a few things that have struck me as I've gone over these accounts.

Please note that all of the following patterns of observation are drawn purely from the accounts of people I have interviewed myself.

- The basics: the creatures are large, covered in hair and bipedal.
- The average height noted by witnesses is between five and seven feet tall. It is well-muscled and generally larger in mass, faster and more powerful than humans.

- The physical features noted include long arms, large hands and feet and a posture slightly different from a human gait or stance, with the most common trait mentioned being a slight bend to the knees and/or a slight tilt forward of the upper body, paraphrasing from one person's description of their stance as kind of leaning forward but not off-balance.
- The body is covered in hair except for portions of the face, the fingers and the bottom surfaces of the hands and feet. The hair is longer than a bear's hair, generally finer in texture and slightly longer in a few regions of the body. Its color is either orange red to mahogany, dark brown with some black coloration in the coat or pure black.
- The area where the head is attached to the shoulders is wide in adults, indicating massive development of the musculature in the equivalent of the human trapezius area. This muscular bulk between head and shoulders fills in area alongside the neck, creating the impression that they have "no neck" in comparison to humans. This area also usually has longer, fuller hair. Immature representatives of the species do not yet demonstrate this musculature, making their heads appear rounder, on top of a more human-proportioned neck.
- The face is partly covered in hair, with dark, pigmented skin exposed above the cheeks. The nose is low profile, with no snout-like appearance. The eyes are large and dark, deep-set under the brow ridge. Some low-light encounters have led to descriptions of a somewhat luminescent quality in bright colors ranging from white to yellow, green or red. The ears are not noticeably visible, perhaps due to hair covering the surrounding area.
- They move quickly and quietly, unless they want to be heard.
- Noises encountered include:
  - A loud, deep roar at a frequency that vibrates any nearby human's sternum bone, frequently triggering a flight response in witnesses.
  - Whistling in imitation of birds or as a more human-like short, sharp signal.
  - Hooting like a large barred owl.
  - Conversational vocalization and grunting.
  - Whooping, short or in series.
  - Knocking of wood and/or rocks, usually heard at a distance.

- They exhibit curiosity about human children, especially when the children are at play or sleeping. In at least one incident of human domestic conflict, protective behavior toward the human child was reported.
- They are seen most often by accident, while in or near the woods, and appear to favor areas with ample water sources, such as rivers, streams, lakes, ponds and swampy areas.
- They give every appearance of having intelligence beyond standard animal intelligence. Most witnesses described the impression that the creatures were too human to be considered just an animal but too animalistic to be considered fully human—somewhere between human and animal, with the attributes and behaviors of both.

As we sift through these accounts and the information that can be gleaned from them, we come up with more and more questions. The only thing I know for sure at this point in my research is that if these creatures are

A boggy area off the backroads of Berwick. *Photo by Michelle Y. Souliere.*

here, they are biological creatures who are our neighbors. We have every obligation to treat them with the same respect we hope they will treat us.

While many of the witnesses I spoke to were terrified by their encounter at the time it occurred, just as many more have since come to feel a sense of ownership and conservatorship in association with the land and its creatures, both big and small, whoever they may be.

Jane Goodall, when questioned about her efforts to aid orphaned chimpanzees, answered with a compelling argument: "Why? Because I value them as individuals. That's what my work has been about. When you meet chimps, you meet individual personalities....We have a responsibility to them."[7]

We have a lot to learn about the world around us still. Let's keep our eyes open.

2
A NOTE ABOUT NATIVE TRIBAL TRADITIONS

Some of you might be disappointed that I am not offering more accounts of Maine Bigfoot in the context of Native American traditions, specifically those of the Wabanaki Confederacy.* This is because the existing recorded accounts of Maine's tribal traditions are all written by outsiders. I do not feel comfortable recounting these writings,† since they are not coming from the tribes themselves.

I know from past experience that historically recorded texts by White folklorists and translators have often misinterpreted the true meanings behind Native traditions, no matter how good their intentions were. I do not want to contribute to that pattern.

I also know that "not all things are meant to be told to everyone or seen."

I made several attempts to contact tribal members and representatives, which have so far been fruitless, and I regret not yet having the time or resources to build a relationship with any of Maine's tribes. I hope that changes in the future, as I believe my understanding of Maine remains woefully incomplete until that happens.

---

* Currently the Wabanaki Confederacy (Waponahki), encompasses five principal nations in Maine and neighboring Canada: the Mi'kmaq, Maliseet, Passamaquoddy, Penobscot and Abenaki.

† Such authors as Frank Speck, Fannie Hardy Eckstorm, Charles Leland, Marion Whitney Smith, Kenneth Morrison, Silas Rand, Elsie Clews Parsons, Garrick Mallery, John E. Roth and others whose works I have read during research for this book, including others whose viewpoints are too condescending to even mention.

Meanwhile, at least a couple of my accounts come from eyewitnesses who wanted their voices to be heard to help others and who identify themselves as tribal members, so there is a natural diversity of representation in the encounters contained herein, even if in their individual accounts they are not identified as such.

My hope for this book is that it creates conversation and understanding between all involved, including the realization that we all see and experience Maine in our own way. Understanding our neighbors' viewpoints is essential to making Maine a better place for everyone who lives here.

3

HISTORICAL ENCOUNTERS THROUGH 1950

No Stranger to These Woods

efore we launch into modern eyewitness accounts, I'd like to quickly tour you through early mentions of Bigfoot-related creatures in Maine. People are often surprised to hear Maine has a history of giants, wildmen and anomalous primates dating to the 1700s. I was surprised myself when I started researching the topic and found ample material for an article that I published in the October 2008 issue of the *Strange Maine Gazette*. While many of these encounters are a far cry from modern eyewitness accounts, they do contain echoes and similarities that investigators will find intriguing.

EARLY ACCOUNTS OF PRIMATE VISITORS

Where does the Maine Bigfoot's lengthy history, and the history of its associated kindred, begin? Earliest records are tentative at best, and even after over a decade of research, I have yet to flesh them out to my satisfaction. However, we have some good starting points.

Maine of the late 1780s was a very different place. In the preceding decades, many settlements had been cleared out in fear, resettled and then cleared out again as territorial wars raged throughout the 1600s and most of the 1700s. The bulk of this unrest ended with the Treaty of Paris in 1763, but upheaval returned with the Revolutionary War before finally ending in 1783. Maine's coastline was a hotbed of patriotic American activity and British conflict during that time. The land saw little in the way of peace and certainly wasn't given time to prosper. Land remained undeveloped. There were few roads and even fewer bridges to assist travelers. Wilderness ruled everything—rocks, forests and waterways.

Digging back to those early days in *Scarborough Becomes a Town* by Dorothy Shaw Libbey,[8] we are tantalized with the following tale of wildmen: "In 1788 there was a general belief in Gorham that certain strange men were wandering about Gorham, Scarborough, and Westbrook. They were called Wildmen. Between the months of July and October it was asserted that there were seen in the fields and in the woods ragged human beings having long, shaggy hair and beards. These people were seen picking berries, green corn, and peas. When they discovered that they were being watched they would run away."

While Libbey cited no source for this material, I tracked it to an earlier book from which she had lifted it: Josiah Pierce's *A History of the Town of Gorham, Maine*[9] and a sizeable appendix article titled simply "Wild Men." I visited the Maine Historical Library in hopes of finding additional notes, but unfortunately (for me), the manuscript is a nice, neat, verbatim copy of what was eventually published as the book itself. I wrote to the current Josiah Pierce, great-great-grandson of Josiah Pierce (1792–1866), hoping he might be able to shed some light, but to his regret, he was unable to help me. His collection of papers included mostly items originating from the family's West Baldwin house. While the historical Josiah had owned that house, he had never lived there. Sadly, today's Josiah did not know of any other repository of Pierce family papers from that generation, either.

Pierce's *A History of the Town of Gorham, Maine* was obviously written with enthusiasm and great regard for the town, and it is equally clear that he felt compelled to include the "Wild Man" section, even if only as a side note. In the closing paragraph of the account, he mentions that he received a written version of these events from "an aged and intelligent gentleman of Gorham." This mystery man "was a boy of ten years of age when these strangers were said to have been seen. [He] fully believed in the truth of the story." Someday I would like to locate that affidavit. We leave Pierce's account behind with perhaps more questions than when we arrived, but we will return to the topic of wildmen later in this chapter.

The second-earliest mention refers to a giant hominid. *An Historical Sketch of Deer Isle, Maine* by George L. Hosmer[10] tells of the discovery, circa 1825, of a huge humanoid skeleton:

> *Occasionally skeletons have been found, and at one time two were discovered under the roots of a large hardwood tree: it had grown to a large size and was in a state of decay, when it was blown over during a storm. One was that of a person of ordinary size, the other of one who was at least eight feet in height, and between the ribs of the larger one was found the head*

of a dart made of copper.* They lay nearly side by side, and had been probably engaged in mortal conflict, the larger one mortally wounded by the smaller, and the smaller probably fell by the hands of the larger.

While Bigfoot enthusiasts might protest that no hairiness is described in the account, the size of the giant remains significant, demonstrating the presence of a larger-than-normal hominid in the distant past of the region.

ENTER THE APES AND MONKEYS

Our next recorded sighting is more traditional, on a smaller scale and one of Maine's most famous historic cases. J.W. McHenri (or McHenry) had his fifteen minutes of fame in 1855 when he wrote to the *Thomaston Journal*, claiming to have captured a small, shrieking, hairy creature while out chopping wood in Waldoboro†:

Mr. Editor: On the morning of January 2d, while engaged [in] *chopping wood a short distance from my house in Waldoboro, I was startled by the most terrific scream that ever greeted my ears; it seemed to proceed from the woods near by. I immediately commenced searching around for the cause of* [this] *unearthly noise, but after a half hour's fruitless search, I resumed my labors, but had scarcely struck a blow with my axe when the sharp shriek bust out upon the air.*

Looking up quickly, I discovered an object about ten rods from me, standing between two trees, which had the appearance of a miniature human being. I advanced towards it, but the little creature fled as I neared it. I gave chase, and after a short run succeeded in catching it. The little fellow turned a most imploring look upon me, and then uttered a sharp shrill shriek, resembling the whistle of an engine.

I took him to my house and tried to induce him to eat some meat, but failed in the attempt. I then offered him some water, of which he drank a small quantity. I next gave him some dried beech nuts, which he cracked and ate readily. He is of a male species, about eighteen inches in height, and his limbs are in perfect proportion. With the exception of his face, hands, and feet, he is covered with hair of a jet black hue.

---

* There are many examples of copper being found at archaeological sites in Maine.

† "A Genuine Native American Know Nothing—A Wild Man in Maine." *Fort Wayne (IN) Sentinel*, January 27, 1855. Please note I have corrected some spelling errors in this version. Every reprinting of this article seemed to have new and interesting misspellings, showing very sloppy presswork. For instance, Trowbridge tavern was alternately spelled as Towbridge, Trobridge, et cetera.

> *Whoever may wish to see this strange specimen of human nature, can gratify their curiosity by calling at my house in the eastern part of Waldoboro, near the Trowbridge tavern. I give these facts to the public to see if there is any one who can account for this wonderful phenomenon.*

The similarity to a monkey is obvious, including the fact that McHenri found it more interested in eating nuts than meat. It seems likely, based on its size, color, diet and the sounds it made, that the little guy was a black spider monkey.[*]

It is not out of the question that monkeys had landed in Maine around this time, due to the state's seafaring legacy of many ports and its sailors' exotic travels.[†] Waldoboro itself is a port town and renowned shipbuilding center, and in 1855, many ships sailed from there carrying (literally) tons of goods all over the world. Trowbridge's Tavern was located on the Warren and Waldoboro post road[11] and had been a local fixture since about 1800, when "Aunt Lydia" Trowbridge opened its doors to the public in a convenient spot near Waltz's Corner.[12]

The origin of this article is elusive, because the *Thomaston Journal* published for only four years and few issues are archived.[13] Luckily for us, in a practice much like AP wire "weird news" articles today, enterprising editors reprinted sensational stories from across the nation. The McHenri article reappeared for weeks after the original date of publication. The most complete reprint I found was in the *Danville Advertiser* from Indiana on March 3, 1855, two full months after the original story ran in Maine.[‡]

A year later, in 1856, an "ape-man's" body, an apparent casualty of a passing train, was found on the tracks near Greenville, Maine, at the southern end of Moosehead Lake. I have not seen this article for myself, so I cannot vouch for its validity. The info was posted by user "Cascade" on Topix.com

---

[*] Joseph Citro, in his excellent book *Passing Strange*, speculates that this creature might have been a Mekumwasuck, held by the local tribes of Passamaquoddy to be "little people," two or three feet tall, whose faces are covered with hair.

[†] For instance, in the *Bangor Daily Whig and Courier* of July 22, 1857, an article discussed the landing of the brig *Flora*, steered by Maine's own Captain Yates of Newcastle. Hailing from the port of Dix Cove on the West Coast of Africa, it made port in New York City, where a monkey on board attracted a curious crowd.

[‡] Other reprints of the article include appearances in *Prescott (WI) Paraclete*, February 14, 1855; *Salem (IN) Democrat*, January 26, 1855; *Hornellsville (NY) Tribune*, January 25, 1855; and *Jackson City Democrat* (Brownstone IN), January 30, 1855. There is also an excellent transcription of the article in Chad Arment's *The Historical Bigfoot* on page 171.

as part of a list of historic Maine sightings.* The lack of documentation for this article remains distracting, but I wanted to include it here for other researchers. I encourage you to contact me if you find the original article.

Monkeys were on Mainers' minds from an early date. In the *Bangor Daily Whig and Courier* of February 25, 1859, Allen H.C. Rice advertised their location in stalls 7 and 9 at the Norombega Market, bragging that they carried, "any thing in our line of business a man could wish for, except the Monkey ALL CHEAPER than can be bought any where else in Bangor." Do you think there was demand for exotic monkey meat in the Bangor area back then?

How many adventurous simians took advantage of a Maine port landing and took shore leave, never to return to their owners? This, perhaps, went on for many years. Certainly, there were traveling exhibits in the state featuring monkeys and apes. The Grand Caravan, for one, came to Bangor on August 11, 1846, at the rear of the Penobscot Exchange with "a large African Baboon and specimens of the Monkey and Ape Tribes."[14]

The very father of the Maine Prohibition Law, Neal Dow, fought a monkey on Portland's wharves as a small child. This remarkable incident is recounted in his memoirs.[15] The event occurred circa 1812 in Portland, Maine, under peculiar circumstances:

> I was…perhaps seven or eight years old, when for some reason that I do not now recollect, I found myself one morning in a barber's shop on Fore street, near the head of one of the wharves.
>
> In a yard connected with the shop was a large monkey, and some of the loiterers there arranged for a fight between the monkey and myself. Not old enough to realize the absurdity of such a match, or to understand that there were only bites and scratches to be had, and no good of any kind, or even so-called honor, to be won from the scrimmage, I permitted myself to be armed with a stout stick furnished by one of the men and entered the territory where the monkey intended to be supreme. The rest of the affair I remember as if it were an occurrence of yesterday.
>
> To such a monkey as I then encountered, it is wise to give a wide berth. He opened the fight with teeth and claw, jumping at my face, biting at me and tearing my clothes with all his considerable might. I kept him in front of me as well as I could, kicking and striking him whenever I got the chance. How long the folly lasted I do not know. For what seemed to me a long time the monkey had most of the fun and I most of the pain, but at

---

* While the Topix.com forums are now defunct, you can view a capture of this page via the Wayback Machine: "Finding Bigfoot in Maine!" East Millinocket, ME, Wayback Machine, https://web.archive.org/web/20080820203557/https://www.topix.com/forum/city/east-millinocket-me/TNUT3RGL25KBGANHT.

length the brute got tired of it and knew enough to give up. Corresponding intelligence on my part would have kept me out of the scrape altogether.

Before I had thrashed the monkey as soundly as I wished, I was called off, and came out of the yard bitten, scratched, bloody and dirty from head to foot, and with clothes torn, but I was so petted and rewarded with candy and round-cakes by the rascally bystanders who had put me up to the fight, that I imagined myself quite a hero until, taking a great deal of the dirt, some of the blood, and all of the scratches home with me, I found, much to my discomfort, that my parents took a very different view of the affair from that held by the barber-shop loafers.

In August 1895, a startling story appeared in the *Bar Harbor Record*,[16] preceding the story of the Durham gorilla by almost eighty years: "People living on the outskirts of South Gardiner have been startled by unearthly shrieks lately. Two women and three boys, who went into the woods for blueberries, came upon a hairy monster which walked upright on his hind legs toward them. They were badly scared, but the animal, which looked like an immense African monkey walked past them, leaving a footprint like a saucer."

The Age of Wildmen and Devils

Mainers encountered and reported wildmen throughout the early years of statehood. Some wildmen settled in a given area as hermits. Some were old neighbors or runaways gone "woods queer." Others were creatures of mystery and terror.

In October 1886, reports came from Waterville of "a terrible wild man" who killed a camper well north of Moosehead Lake (presumably at or just over the Canadian border) and suffered the same fate himself at the hands of a posse.[17] Clearly the catch v. kill decision was not a big issue, as made clear in the article's title:

A New Kind of Game
An affrighted Frenchman from over the line has his fellows in town all by the ears with a story of a gigantic wild man, killed a week or so ago in the dense woods above Moosehead. The Frenchman's story, which is implicitly believed, is that three men were camping out in the woods about a hundred miles north of Moosehead Lake. Two of the campers were away from the camp for a week and came back to find the dead body of their companion. They went for help and reinforced by a dozen others searched the woods for the unknown murderer. It proved to be a terrible wild man, ten feet tall, with

arms seven feet in length, covered with long, brown hair. The party fired several shots into him and finally succeeded in reaching a vital spot, laying the monster low.

This story was reprinted in many newspapers across the country and originally seemed too good to be true, as discussed between Loren Coleman, Chuck Flood and myself, since they were appearing in newspapers conveniently far away from Maine over several months. (The story reappeared in the May 5, 1887 issue of the *Los Angeles Times*, as well as earlier in the *Eau Clair Daily Free Press* of November 9, 1886.) But in 2013, *Bangor Daily News* reporter Nok-Noi Ricker printed an article featuring a contemporary clipping from another Bangor publication, and that laid our worries to rest.[18]

Almost a decade later came November 1895's "A TERROR IN THE WOODS." Another vicious wildman was alarming lumber camps in the north woods. Over two months, men disappeared one by one. When found in the woods, their bodies were "terribly mangled and torn." The wildman attacked one man who was out working alone with his axe, which he used to fend off the fiend. Following this, the wildman was periodically spotted by crews, "but on their approach he fled into the deep woods with the speed of a deer."

A Bangor report stated, "He is described as being so nearly like an animal that it is almost impossible to detect him from one. He has a long, shaggy beard, and is covered with a huge, skin coat."[19] It was thought that he was a lost hunter gone "hopelessly crazy." Questing lumber crews hoped to shoot him in the leg to allow capture.

In December 1895, the *Bar Harbor Record* reported that "a man thought to be the wild man of Scarboro Marsh [*sic*], near Portland, was found Friday in a hovel eating a broiled cat."[20] Interested readers will note 1895 was the year of the Winstead, Connecticut Wildman, a famous case of the time that caused a flap of wildman references and sightings countrywide.

In July 1896, the Wildman of Minot was frequenting woods near Minot and South Auburn. The encounters had hallmarks of traditional Bigfoot encounters, including "noise like the breaking of [tree] limbs," and encounters with the hairy character while blueberrying.[21] Unlike Bigfoot, he was naked, bearded and sometimes jumped out and yelled at horse-driven carriages. A search party of about one hundred people was formed to no avail. Speculation was rampant regarding which local missing man he might be, but none seemed likely.

By early August 1896, he appeared to a startled farmer "clad in tattered clothes, with a long butcher knife in his waist band." That farmer was Councilman John Stinchfield of Auburn, and he recounted his experience to the press in great detail.[22] We can already see some protocols still associated with Bigfoot reporting, in reassurances that our witness is an honorable man: "Now, first of all it should be known that Mr. Stinchfield is a man of mature years, a prosperous and well-known farmer, a councilman in the Auburn city government and a man whose honesty and character are unquestionably of the best. He doesn't seek notoriety but when any one asks him about the report that he saw a wild man he just tells the story."

It was also clear that this wildman was a human male, not a monster (although likely a maniac—that long butcher knife certainly gave Councilman Stinchfield some pause). Stinchfield said, "I asked all the questions I could think of but nary an answer would he give me. He didn't utter a word. All he did was to stand there and stare at me. He had a wild look in his eyes and I set him down as an Insane man....I wasn't much frightened at the time. I took in the situation and decided it best for me to stand my ground. If I had run he might have followed me."

The wildman was first sighted by Miss Maud Knowlton of Minot.[23] In response, the *Mechanic Falls Ledger* received a letter from Mrs. J.W. Wilder of Washburn, hoping that similarities between the wildman and her brother Aaron Learned, missing since autumn 1895, meant he had finally been found. She forwarded a photo of her brother to Knowlton, but so far as I can ascertain, no positive identification occurred. Those years produced myriad wildmen of one sort or another, and one hopes they all found warm places to hide by winter, a harsh mistress once summer's fancy has flown the Maine countryside.

In June 1898, speculation was raised by complaints to Bath police regarding strange occurrences near Witch Spring.[24] Two ladies driving past were pursued by a man who ran out of the woods wearing only an undershirt. A West Bath farmer reported hearing yells in the woods nearby. Officers were unable to capture the culprit. An article of the prior decade mentions various reasons for the spring's name: "Some have claimed it to have been so called from the fact that ghosts, hobgoblins, and witches made it a resort."[25] It certainly seems to have historically attracted odd behavior, if nothing else.

These news items were opportunities for enterprising editors to comment on local politics. On page 1 of the same issue of the *Bath Independent*, the Gobbles column read: "Speaking of that Witch Spring wild man, when you consider the tax bills sent Bathites year after year it's rather remarkable that the suburban forests aren't full of wild men!"*

---

* And the 1895 Scarboro wildman account (see above, *Bar Harbor Record*, December 1895) prompted a similar response commentary on a mysterious food favorite of Bangorians, called Frankfort sausage.

In July 1905, Poland's Wild Man blew the minds of locals when he arrived.[26] Locals were fed up with this phenomenon but willing to use it for sport. The wildman's "mysterious actions" were described in terms that announced he was a threat. "He tried to kill one man by throwing a railroad iron at him and startled two families by throwing stones through the windows….He carries a railroad iron, such as is used in coupling cars. On the end of it is a bouquet of wild flowers. This he brandishes as his war club."

On Saturday, about fifty men searched the countryside for him, to no avail. Women at home alone locked doors and windows, and large dogs were a popular accoutrement. Surrounding towns were warned. But most telling in these articles is the offhand commentary in between the facts:

> *Mr. A.B. Ricker of the Poland Spring House has made every plan to capture the man and reports of his capture are expected every minute. Some of the young men and boys at Poland Spring have joined in the hunt. They like no better sport than hunting a wild man in the Maine woods. The wild man has come in the height of the summer season to furnish sensations for the sojourners at our summer resorts. Since the sea serpent washed ashore at Old Orchard…there has been nothing out of the ordinary to interest them.*

All joking aside, there was serious speculation that excessive heat had affected his brain, and taking no chances, all berrying parties in the town were postponed. Early the next week, he was caught when he rode into Portland on top of a Pullman railroad car, and he was identified as Peter E. Harding of Lewiston.[27]

In May 1907, Riggsville had its turn[28] with a "stranger" who "has been heard to creep through the underbrush and thickets and seems to have a natural fondness for gulleys and swamps, and some people tell of seeing him from a distance as he has jumped and leaped to get out of sight of human visage."

In late summer 1913, there was a flare-up in Durham, but by September, the "wildman" was attributed to a group of families protecting their blueberry patch from invading berry enthusiasts.[29] Described as a "primitive nut" who spent part of August that year larking about the fields and woods "with nothing to cover his identity but bushes and his ability to evade all searchers," the wildman's presence served its purpose. "Berry picking picnics were postponed. Nobody dared enter the wood or pastures. The effect on the berry bushes was as had been planned, and the schemers harvested the fruits of their prevarications." Was this true? Or was this just a way to pan the story, dismissing and shelving it, eliminating future discussion? We'll probably never know. As late as October, locals were still joking about it, and travelers continued to keep an eye out for him.[30]

Back to Bigfoot

The next account emerges from the Meddybemps area in Washington County, circa 1940, at best guess.[31] Jackson and Tulane Porter reported hearing this tale recounted by two elder women from the Indian Township Reservation at a Thanksgiving dinner in 2006. (He estimated their age at eighty-plus years and thought the events might have happened about sixty years previous as a result.)

The two women went on family camping trips when they were young, and a sound would sometimes arise at night, wailing across the dark lake water. "They explained the howling was more like a monotonous singing from someone with a husky voice, but it was called a howler." At a favorite fishing spot after sunset, the girls found themselves alone as the howling started. They turned to see two "black giants" staring down at them. The bigger one took the day's catch from the girls' bucket and then walked over to the smaller giant and handed the fish over. They returned to the water and swam away with their heisted dinner.

The beings were described by the women as "two-fathers high" and "covered in black shiny hair.…[They] had huge hairy black hands with fingers as big as the fish [we] caught [smallmouth bass]. They had big feet and had on no clothing." This last detail caused them much amusement, even sixty-plus years later. When their parents arrived later to pick them up by canoe, they appeared unsurprised by the girls' story. The "Meddybemps howler" was familiar to them and known to steal fish "and sometimes little girls." They never fished that spot again.

Tyler M. Smith, posting in response to this account at the same site, adds further tales from his great aunt about what he thinks were the same creatures: "My great aunt tells me her sister, my grandmother now passed, talked about that same Meddybemps creature and told one story where two of them threw rocks at fisherman [*sic*] on the lake and sometimes stormed the canoes, swamping them by churning up the water and screaming. She thinks this must have been around 1942. There was another account of the Meddybemps howler scaring children bathing in the lake by swimming up underneath them, lifting them out of the water and dropping them back into the water."

Another tantalizing online account is from Mount Bigelow, near Sugarloaf Mountain, mentioned by Bobbie Short's Bigfoot Encounters site.* It has to do with dowsers (a topic for yet another book), and since it is a curiosity in the pre-Patterson-Gimlin era, readers might find it of interest, as I do. I'm including another Bigelow area sighting from the site as well:

> *1946—Bigelow Mountain. Four dowsers were startled when they stopped along a trail to eat lunch and instead saw an enormous man walking toward them in the distance that was well over ten feet tall. He had long hair like Indians in movies & was covered in short black hair over the rest of his body. He carried what looked like a big rock. They left the area immediately.*

> *1949—Bigelow Mountain. 150 miles northwest of Augusta, Maine. A man named Burn White saw a 7-foot creature standing on the side of the road at 1 A.M. Another person reported seeing the same creature at an earlier date.*

Known accounts on record after this point enter the realm of awareness in the era following release of the Patterson-Gimlin footage in October 1967, which created a major breaking point between a relatively unknown phenomenon and the threshold of a wider awareness about Sasquatch/Bigfoot in general.

In the late 1950s, stories began circulating on the West Coast about Sasquatch sightings, and the first modern Bigfoot hunters began to track the creature, but it took a long time for these tales to spread. What started in the 1950s slowly built in volume until the Patterson-Gimlin footage blew the story up to epic proportions, and the whole country heard about it. While most folks still didn't expect to see Bigfoot themselves, by the early 1970s, most Americans had at least heard about the monster if they watched television, read books and newspapers or went to the movies.†

---

* "Historic Sasquatch Sightings: Maine," Bigfoot Encounters, http://www.bigfootencounters.com. This site is a terrific resource, but Bobbie Short rarely cited her sources, which leaves us little to go on after her death. Her friend Chris Millet maintains the site now but does not have any of her research material handy (per email conversation in April 2019).

† The interim Maine sightings from this midcentury period are fairly well documented through various sources online, and if you prefer a paper and ink version, they can also be found in the source documents quoted in Green, *Shadows in the Woods* (see chapter 8, Bigfoot Encounters).

PART II

EYEWITNESS TESTIMONY
(CHRONOLOGICAL)

4

TALKING WITH EYEWITNESSES

We now move into the present-day and recent past. In early 2016, I shifted gears and began recording the current oral history of Maine Bigfoot sightings, focusing on events that were important to record before being lost to time. From the start of this project, I followed a strong hunch that there are a lot of accounts here in Maine that have not been recorded yet. To be honest, I was not expecting much response. Mainers generally aren't going to blab about this stuff. This is the kind of thing people talk about with close friends and family, if anyone at all.

Most people who volunteered to talk with me had similar motivations:

- They wanted to find out if I had talked to other people who had experiences like theirs or had experiences near where theirs had occurred.
- They wanted to put their encounter on record in case it could help others.
- They wanted to positively influence perception of these creatures in case their existence becomes a matter of public information.

Many had no explanation for their encounter. However, they knew the details might be significant to someone else, either because that person knew more about the subject and could glean information from their account or because that person was wondering about their own inexplicable experiences too.

Many of my interviewees had no prior interest in Bigfoot or Sasquatch phenomena, beyond a passing exposure to the topic, similar to most folks who grew up in the 1960s and 1970s.

Many cited the recent television show *Finding Bigfoot* as a source of reassurance. After watching the show, they realized they weren't the only people who had this type of experience and that not everyone was going to treat them with disbelief and ridicule. It was also validating to find out there are people dedicating themselves to investigating similar encounters. *Finding Bigfoot* let them know they were not alone.

In some cases, this realization came after decades of feeling separated from even their family and friends by a single moment in time, by that one shocking experience.

With a few exceptions, their encounters occurred accidentally. They were somewhere at the same time something else traveled through that location. They crossed paths with it. This type of sighting is momentary, often lasting only a few seconds, yet for the rest of their lives, the memory vividly remains.

Over the years, they find themselves returning again and again to that puzzle—what did they see? And like a puzzle piece, they turn the memory over and over in their minds, trying to fit it into familiar boxes. Was it a bear? Was it a moose? Was it a person? Every time, the answer is no, and they are left holding that piece of memory, with nowhere to put it but in the back of their minds, where it continues to stand, alone and strange.

Most sightings outside the single-encounter category have to do with proximity of habitat—in other words, the eyewitness lives in a location adjoining territory inhabited or passed through regularly by the creature. In some of these events, the creatures appear to exhibit curiosity about humans when they encounter them, especially in the case of children.

The funny thing about this book is that even though it is now officially "finished," this subject looks like it will remain a lifelong pursuit for me.

Why? You may well ask.

Because there are more encounters out there, untold outside a small circle of family and friends. I can feel it in my bones. Because each link that appears in the chain of Maine oral history strengthens everyone who is part of it. Because these accounts stand ready for those who come after, for those who have not told their own history yet, for those who might think no one wants to hear this or that people are just going to think they're crazy or an idiot.

I've heard a lot of reasons from people about why they don't want to come forward.

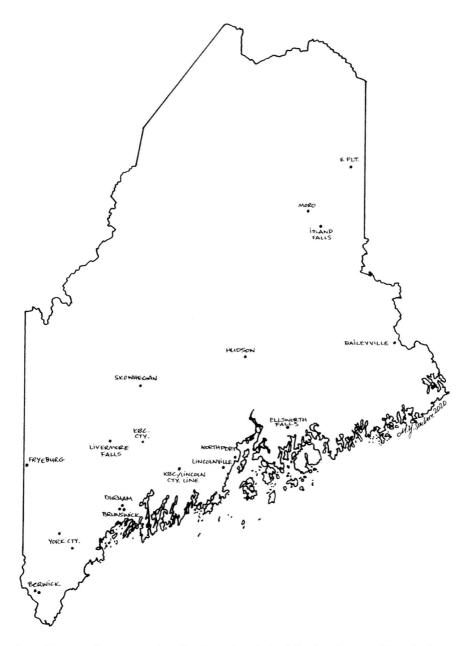

Statewide map of encounters based on interviews in the following chapters. *Illustration by Michelle Y. Souliere.*

It's okay to keep things to yourself. But if you have an encounter that defies your prior life experience, something that doesn't fit into your known universe, I want you to know that there are those of us who will listen.

If we are honorable, ethical journalists (or even friends), we will listen off the record. We won't tell anyone what you don't want known. The information is still useful, even when we keep it confidential. You would be surprised to hear some of the tiny clues that have led me to huge breakthroughs and realizations.

We will listen, whether you want the details shared to help others in the same boat or if you require us to never tell another soul. We will not assign you derogatory labels just because something happened to you that we haven't experienced ourselves. And those of us who look at the bigger picture will be grateful and remember what you shared with us when you didn't have to share anything at all.

You might not hear from us again for years—or ever—but know that your piece of the puzzle is percolating through a repository of Maine history. We each have our own unique experience of this state and everything in it. Without each other, we are less. Don't think your shot in the dark has been ignored. These things take time.

In those moments when your piece of the puzzle fills in a blank, connecting other pieces together, it helps create an amazing picture of Maine history, rich treasure for those who come later, asking questions only we can answer now.

Our work is done with no promise of glory, no promise of tangible results. Those of us who listen, who dig deep when everyone else is doing something they think is more fun—we are looking long. We are looking ahead as well as looking behind.

We are also trying to get as close as we can to a 360-degree view, because things only become clear with perspective. We never know what to expect, and that's a good thing. We make no definite predictions—we lay out our cards, pay attention and hope to see things unfold.

And for those who shy away from telling because they have seen others' stories exploited by those who don't care about anything but profit and personal gain, I am sorry this behavior exists. It is unnecessary and violates everything I stand for. I respect your decision to back away from opening up because you have seen others injured in doing so.

To those who trusted me with their experiences, thank you. I came to you a stranger, and you were willing to take a chance that I could help other people with your accounts. This means a tremendous amount to me and to others who will now read about your experiences. I am lucky you all looked at me or heard my voice or saw my greeting on the screen and said, "OK. I will give you a try."

5

SUZY

Hairy Man: A Childhood Encounter

KENNEBEC COUNTY
CIRCA 1963–70

While most of my interviewees were contacted via phone or email, Suzy requested we do things differently. She preferred to meet me in person, "because you can tell a lot about a person by looking in their eyes." Suzy contacted me after Lincoln County Television (LCTV) aired a half-hour documentary titled *Hairy Man: My Life with Big Foot,* in which she was interviewed by producer Bruce Hilsmeyer.[32]

I watched the documentary several times. It was compelling and well made, without sensationalizing an explosive topic. It is simply a person talking about experiences that seem unbelievable but, nevertheless, were a formative experience in her life. Suzy chose to go on record partly out of concern for the increase in Bigfoot trophy hunters who aim to capture or kill a specimen for profit and because of distressingly negative depictions of Bigfoot. She reminds us they are a fellow species, existing alongside us very privately, meaning us no harm.

This account relates a multi-year run of Class A and Class B sightings.*

---

* A Class A sighting is one in which persons have "clear sightings in circumstances where misinterpretation or misidentification of other animals can be ruled out with greater confidence." A Class B sighting delineates "incidents in any other circumstance that did not afford a clear view of the subject." For a full list of classification types, see "BFRO Database History and Report Classification System," Bigfoot Field Researchers Organization, http://www.bfro.net.

IT WAS JANUARY 2018 when I hopped on the Downeaster Amtrak train to meet Suzy. Unable to get her permission to record our interview, I tried to take accurate notes as we talked.* Suzy estimates that she "was probably about five or six years old the first time I felt that maybe there was something watching me."[33]

Her family had moved to a very rural setting, a road that only had two or three year-round residences. Their house was set back from the road, overlooking a lake. During cocktail parties, her mother would keep an eye on her through the window while hostessing. Suzy felt something watching her while she played alone. One night, she caught a glimpse of something hairy but then it was gone. Later, she saw it again. It was around seven feet tall with long hands, standing at the edge of the woods, watching her. She did not feel threatened.

The hairy man, or Wabou', as she called him, kept his distance at first. They developed a communication system involving calls, knocks and grunts so that she could tell him when she was outside. Time went by. Wabou' brought his mate and their child, about Suzy's own size, to visit.

She remembers wading in the lake during summer. By age nine or ten, she was often unattended. Sometimes Wabou' would wade in with her. He noticed she couldn't swim yet. Once he nudged her into the water, and when she dunked over her head, "the next thing I know I'm being pulled up. Everything happened so fast. He put me on top of his shoulders and then threw me into the water and was looking at me going like this." In the LCTV video interview, Suzy mimics a reaching, paddling motion with her arms. "So, I just started doing this and ended up coming back towards him. I didn't go under.…I managed to keep my head above water…and went back over to him, and I crawled on top of his shoulders again…and then he would lunge forward, and I'd fall off. That's how I learned to swim."

When Suzy tried to mention this to her mother, she was told to stop making up stories. Suzy never told anyone else, assuming she wouldn't be believed. Even Suzy's husband of many years had only the tiniest inkling until she told her story on camera while he sat nearby, hearing her full story for the first time. She certainly didn't want to raise the topic with her stepfather back then. "I didn't really have a good relationship with him. I was scared of him. Because he drank a lot. He hollered." One of her most vivid memories is of a time when her stepfather was scared off by Wabou':

---

* This is why most of the longer quotes in this chapter come from the documentary. I don't want to misquote her. Much of what we talked about in person referred to and augmented the material in the LCTV interview.

One night my stepfather got drunk, and I was outside playing. It was pretty near dark. He came over and grabbed me, and said, "I told you to get in the house now!*" All of a sudden, I heard* BANG! BANG! *There was a tree limb that hit the side of the house. You could hear a window break. It hit the back door with such force that it broke the door. He just dropped me where I was and ran, stumbled over himself to get back to the house. Just left me there. But it was the hairy man, and he just looked at me and grunted.*

Suzy believes Wabou' was telling her stepfather to back off, telling him not to hurt her. She theorizes that most people encounter male Bigfoot, who are more protective and territorial from her experience, and the ones in charge of traveling to forage for food.

Around the age of twelve, Suzy and her mother moved houses following a violent blowout with her stepfather. There was only enough time to pack and load the car the next morning, fleeing while her stepfather remained passed out. Her last contact with Wabou' was the night before, when she fled into the woods for comfort during the height of the altercation. Wabou' had never seen her like this, gripped by fear, tears and emotions boiling over. His female mate rocked back and forth, distressed. Wabou' reacted by picking things up from the ground and throwing them at the house. Not knowing what else to do, they embraced Suzy to comfort her. Early the next morning, she slipped back inside without realizing it was her last chance to say goodbye to her adoptive family.

I talked to Suzy, the two of us perched in comfy café window seats, sunlit and warm in the January afternoon. Both on screen and in person, Suzy is a very sincere, direct person. One of our first interactions started with her asking me, "So, are you interested only in fiction regarding Strange Maine? Or facts?" Facts, please! I wanted to know more. All those years alongside the hairy man and his family gave her a rare chance to observe them on a regular basis. I had plenty of questions for her.

We discussed their eating habits. In the video, she mentioned they would eat hornpout (catfish, also known as Brown Bullheads, *Ameiurus nebulosus*)[34] and sunfish out of the lake. They loved the lake algae, but local camp owners treated the lake with bleach or other poisons to clear the water and hasten the natural process of the lake each spring when it "flipped." Anything from the bottom of the lake was good eating, including freshwater clams, even dead fish; they seemed to enjoy the added gaminess. When she went to visit the location recently with author Linda Godfrey, they talked to the current owner of the house, who had wondered about the stacks of emptied clam shells he found regularly on the lake shore.[35] Ripe berries were a sweet seasonal treat. Old cigarettes had their burnt ends snapped off and were eaten, "paper and all."[36] She saw them kill small animals for meat, which she told me "is not part of the fairy tale version that people want to hear."

Their hair changed with the seasons. In summer it was a lighter, brownish red, deepening toward a mahogany color in the winter, with fine long hair growing longest between neck and head. The hair of their undercoat is almost fluffy when seen on its own. During the winter, the hair on their faces increases.

Their eyes are round, not oval like the human eye tends to be. She doesn't recall seeing the whites of their eyes, just darkness under their brows. An interesting quality she mentioned is that their eyes give off a red glow at night, allowing her to locate Wabou' even in complete darkness. Their skin is dark and brown—heavily pigmented, very unlike Caucasian skin tone. The heel, sole and sides of their feet are free of hair. They appear flat-footed, with no noticeable arch. Their hands are very large, with long fingers. They are tall but not outlandishly so; she remembers Wabou' and his mate being six to seven feet tall.

Their vocalizations vary from a deep roar to conversational or inquiring noises, including the grunts she and Wabou' used to communicate. They move quickly and silently, unless trying to intimidate. They regularly travel distances for important things like food.

She remembers realizing at about nine or ten years old, "I was old enough to know that this wasn't an animal. It, I thought, was more like a human, only it was a very *big* human. But it *wasn't* a human….Because at that age, I knew then that they weren't something that was a normal thing you saw."

At the close of her LCTV video interview, when asked by Mr. Hilsmeyer if she wanted to give any final remarks, she added that people ought not to fear them. Their life should be respected like any other life. "I think [humans] need to back off on the notion to shoot one to gain fame….It may not be a human life, but it's a life." Her closing advice to viewers was this:

> If you're fortunate enough to have one, or a clan, in your life, try and learn from them. Don't harm them. If you bring them things like food or tobacco, they'll bring you something back, and it may not be an object, it may be knowledge. With me and my experiences, it was more knowledge that they

gave me as gifts than anything else....I don't think that I would have made it through all that I've been through in my life...if I didn't have those experiences with the hairy man when I was younger....He implanted that instinct in me to survive.

As we wrapped up our discussion, the first of more to come, Suzy drove me back to the train depot, leaving me with a lot to think about.

6

TAMMY SAIRIO

The Durham Gorilla: A Menagerie of Mystery and the Curse of Infamy

DURHAM-BRUNSWICK TOWN LINE AREA, CUMBERLAND AND ANDROSCOGGIN
COUNTIES
JULY 25–31, 1973

The sightings known as the Durham Gorilla or Durham Ape events occurred over a few days in summer 1973, near the town line between Brunswick and Durham, Maine. For such a short window in time, the repercussions echo still. It is easily Maine's most famous Bigfoot-associated case. With fame comes trouble, and though the story has been widely repeated, details seem as murky today as they did over forty-five years ago.

I wrote this chapter last, convinced that the infamous tale was not the whole story. I wanted this chapter to come out of the shadows of that warm July afternoon and let me get a better look at it, so you all could see it too. Despite my best efforts, this story remains incomplete.

The first eyewitnesses on record were Lois Huntington, age thirteen; her friend Tammy Sairio,* age twelve; and Lois's two younger brothers, George Huntington Jr., age ten, and Scott Huntington, age eight. The chronology of known events are as follows, based on newspapers reports of the time. Please see complete list of articles at chapter end. To condense the notes in this chapter but still give future researchers an easy key for following the unfolding of this convoluted storyline, abbreviations of newspaper names are used in this section: *Biddeford-Saco Journal* (*BSJ*), *Brunswick Times-Record* (*BTR*), *Portland Evening Express* (*EE*), *Lewiston Daily Sun* (*LDS*), *Lewiston Evening Journal* (*LEJ*), *Maine Sunday Telegram* (*MST*), *Portsmouth Herald* (*PH*) and *Portland Press Herald* (*PPH*).

---

* Tammy's name was misspelled throughout newspaper accounts. The spelling of her last name was Sairio, not Sairo.

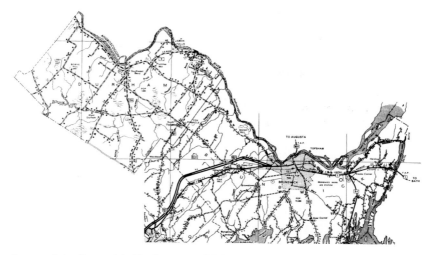

A map of the Brunswick/Durham area. Maine General Highway Atlas, *1959*.

Wednesday July 25, 1973

Early afternoon: Two kids report seeing a "monster" on Durham Road near the Brunswick town line (*LDS*, 7/27/73, 27). Later articles correct total to four kids, and further accounts mention names Lois Huntington, Scott Huntington and George Huntington Jr., with houseguest and friend Tammy Sairio (*PPH*, 7/28/73, 15).

Mr. George Huntington calls police to report the incident (*MST*, 7/29/73, 1).

Later reports state, "Police found probably moose tracks, and wrote it off as a matter of mistaken identity" (*PPH*, 7/27/73, 18).

Thursday July 26, 1973

Around 7:15 p.m., Neota Huntington, driving home from a baseball game, reports seeing an "ape" peeking from bushes on Durham Road at Brunswick town line. "She coasted her car slowly so as not to scare it," but it runs into the woods (*LDS*, 7/27/73, 2). Later account mentions that George Jr. was with her (*MST*, 7/29/73, 24A).

At home, Neota tells her husband. He calls Deputy Sheriff Blaine Footman. Footman calls the Androscoggin Sheriff's Department, "and a number of deputies were dispatched to the scene," plus game wardens and Cumberland County deputies. State police are notified (*LDS*, 7/27/73, 2).

SEARCH BEGINS (*BSJ*, 7/27/73, 1). Neota gathers neighbors and returns to search. She reports seeing it again "peering" through crotch of tree and then vanishing (*PPH*, 7/28/73, 15).

Police join search. "Over 30 police cars" are dispatched from nearby towns, according to Auburn Dog officer Louis Pinette (*LEJ*, 7/27/73, 2). Another article reports "about 20 police and sheriff's deputies" involved in the "two-hour search," including officers from Brunswick, Lisbon Falls and Freeport and deputy sheriffs from both Cumberland and Androscoggin Counties. State police join the scene (*PPH*, 7/27/73, 18).

Police dispatcher reports dozens of calls late Thursday from "concerned residents…after radio reports suggested that an ape might be on the loose near Brunswick" (*PPH*, 7/27/73, 18). Reports air on local television (*PPH*, 7/28/73, 15). Police patrol area through the night, convinced animal is "a bear, possibly standing erect to eat berries" (*PPH*, 7/27/73, 18).

Search party reports no traces found that evening. Neota Huntington states neighbors found only a rotten stump torn apart as though some animal was searching for grubs. No gardens reported disturbed. No other sightings reported besides Neota's on this date (*PPH*, 7/28/73, 15). She describes creature as "about five feet four inches tall, with a shaggy, black coat and weighing about 350 pounds" (*LDS*, 7/27/73, 2).

Friday July 27, 1973
SEARCH CONTINUES (*BSJ*, 7/27/72, 1). Navy helicopter survey of area in late morning reveals nothing but rabbits. Police Chief Favreau mentions leads on possible owner of hypothetical missing ape/monkey. Favreau states police will investigate local gorilla costumes (*BTR*, 7/27/73, 1, 9).

Footprints found in cemetery by Peter and Jean Merrill. Tracks are photographed and plaster cast made (*LDS*, 7/28/73, 2). Animal Control officer Pinette reports finding "fresh tracks which are too big to be those of a bear and which indicate the animal weighs at least 300 pounds" (*EE*, 7/27/73, 4).

Police clamp down on persons with guns entering wooded search area (*BTR*, 7/30/73, 1, back page). "A constant stream of cars patrolled" the normally quiet road, and spectators parked alongside the woods "in hope of seeing the creature" (*PPH*, 7/28/73, 15).

Neota Huntington reports taking "some overripe bananas to the area Friday in the hope that the animal will find them" (*PPH*, 7/28/73, 15).

Saturday July 28, 1973
Portland Press Herald now refers to the creature as a chimpanzee instead of a gorilla. Theories of an abandoned animal are mentioned. Public is reminded that it "appears not to be dangerous." Neota Huntington describes it as "about five feet tall, weighing 300 to 350 pounds and covered with shaggy black fur" and "standing upright" and running on two legs (*PPH*, 7/28/73, 15).

Sunday July 29, 1973

Neota Huntington wishes she never told anyone, due to resulting ridicule (*MST*, 7/29/73, 1). Lois Huntington tells her version of story, saying she and her brothers "looked up simultaneously to see a shaggy creature walking upright through a little cemetery by the side of the road. 'At first I thought it was a man running across the graveyard,' she said. 'Me and Tammy and Junior rode right over to see what it was'" (*MST*, 7/29/73, 24A).

Androscoggin County deputy sheriff Blaine Footman reports he has "come across some signs he considers unusual," including the "rather deep footprint," which was plaster cast and mentioned previously, "definitely not a bear track." Footman declines to speculate on what is going on (*MST*, 7/29/73, 1).

Carlton L. Merrill, owner of a local exotic animal farm, mentions that three months ago in Lisbon Falls someone "had an old male chimp in the back of a station wagon and he was trying to give it away…and maybe decided to dump it." He mentions a mature chimp that is well-fed could weigh 250 pounds (*MST*, 7/29/73, 24A).

Monday July 30, 1973

SEARCH RELAXED (*BTR*, 7/30/73, 1, back page). Police accompany volunteer dowser to woods in the area of the original sighting, with no results (*BTR*, 7/31/73, back page).

The only newspaper to later report Monday morning sighting of "ape-like figure" is *Portland Press Herald*. The figure was standing on Rossmore Road (about six miles from original sighting), seen by Alden Williams. On seeing Williams's car, the figure "ran into the woods." It ran "just like a man." Five police officers and two coastal wardens arrive minutes after sighting and find no evidence in nearby woods (*PPH*, 7/31/73, 17).

Brunswick Times Record calls attention to rumors of Lisbon Falls man known to own a chimpanzee and drive around with it in his station wagon. Drapeau's missing gorilla costume is mentioned too (*BTR*, 7/30/73, 1, back page).

Tuesday July 31, 1973

Corrinne Drapeau from Drapeau's Costumes in Lewiston tells police that a gorilla costume rented in early July under a false name and address has not been returned (*LDS*, 7/31/73, 28). Drapeau's missing gorilla costume is stated as the official cause of sightings by Brunswick Police captain Lawrence Joy. Police state a photo of a model in the costume is being shown to eyewitnesses (*BTR*, 7/31/73, back page).

Portland Press Herald reports police now suspect hoax in one edition, while other editions have no mention of case at all. Captain Lawrence W. Joy states that "he has suspected a hoax from the start." He mentions "someone in a gorilla costume was wandering around the downtown area in May to advertise a 'freaker's ball' rock concert to be held the following day at White's Beach." Police are attempting to trace gorilla costumes in the area (*PPH*, 7/31/73, 17). It is stated that the Drapeau's costume has been missing since March (conflicting with LDS article) (*PPH*, 7/31/73, 17).

Theory of publicity stunt is raised. James Freeman, manager of local drive-in theater where *The Battle for the Planet of the Apes* showed the prior week "disclaims any responsibility for it" (*PPH*, 7/31/73, 17). *Lewiston Daily Sun* publishes costume-related article and mentions someone in a gorilla costume coming out of Lisbon Falls market about a month earlier, getting into a small foreign car and driving away (*LDS*, 7/31/73, 28).

Wednesday August 1, 1973
A brief article about the costume is the only mention of the case, appearing in New Hampshire's *Portsmouth Herald* (*PH*, 8/1/73, 17).

THIS IS THE STORY as pieced together via eighteen articles spread across nine different newspapers in Maine, New Hampshire and Massachusetts over the course of a week. I spent hours scouring microfilm reels at the Portland Room (Portland Public Library) and sifting through online archives. I was lucky enough to gain the kind assistance of Lynne Holland, who went above and beyond in searching Curtis Memorial Library's *Times Record* newspaper archives in Brunswick. From this hodgepodge of resources, over several years of research, I managed to assemble many articles about the incident.

The articles are a crazy quilt of information, speculation and typos. Shockingly, none of the articles seems to tell the full narration of the children's encounter. Even Loren Coleman's official Bigfoot Research Organization (BFRO) report covers only the basic fact that the children saw the creature.[*]

I tried to track down the major eyewitnesses. It took me a long time to work myself up to contact them. If you've ever tried to cold call someone who probably doesn't want to talk to you, then you know why. When I finally

---

[*] The report by Loren Coleman can be found on the BFRO website as "Report # 1186," BFRO, January 1, 1998, http://www.bfro.net; re-posted at "Durham Gorilla Revisited," Cryptomundo, August 2, 2011, https://cryptomundo.com.

dialed the first number, I thought I had struck out. I started leaving a message on the answering machine but was surprised by a voice on the other end. I was talking to Sandi, wife of George Huntington Jr. She politely but firmly let me know George was no longer interested in talking to anyone about the "Bigfoot thing." The family had talked to reporters in the past, and every time, she said, "They don't seem to want to know the truth."

I explained my historical approach. She paused and gave me an interesting clue. There had been a wildlife farm near the sightings. She and George thought that it probably had an illegal gorilla.* It had gotten loose, scared the neighborhood and resulted in the Huntingtons being ridiculed their whole lives because they reported what they'd seen, and it was classified as a Bigfoot sighting forevermore.

The owner of the farm, she recalled, was named Carleton Merrill. No reporters checked this information when the Huntingtons told them about it. "Nobody wanted to hear the truth because they just wanted the Bigfoot story." Now all the family wanted to do was to put it behind them. I thanked her, and we said our farewells. Next I tried Scott Huntington's number, and after initially getting a busy signal, I was greeted by a message saying the number was disconnected. It was pretty clear they didn't want to discuss the encounter anymore, and I could hardly blame them. Sadly, there was no way to talk to Neota, their mother, as she passed away in 2010, or their sister Lois, who predeceased Neota in 2004.

While I worked up the gumption to try contacting the last of the eyewitnesses, I did more research. Thanks to Sandi giving me a name to work from, a few things emerged. The first was a 1976 article describing the

---

* In 1973, changes in Maine legislation made many primates illegal to keep in the state, a reflection of growing interest in animal conservation worldwide, and an attempt to curtail black market animal trade. It seemed the possibility of someone attempting to dispose of a now-illegal ape should be explored. The timing seemed too close to be a coincidence. However, it turned out that the Endangered Species Act wasn't signed into effect by President Nixon until December 28, 1973—five months after the Durham Gorilla occurrences. "Endangered and Threatened Species," Maine Field Office—Ecological Services, U.S. Fish & Wildlife Service, https://www.fws.gov.

It should also be noted that even after this significant change, there were plenty of loopholes, so savvy collectors and dealers could find a way around the list of prohibited species, especially primates: "Certain individual apes that were held in captivity (for noncommercial purposes) at the time that their species was listed as 'endangered' (known as 'pre-act wildlife') may be freely imported, exported, and transferred for non-commercial purposes. For example, a person that has kept an orangutan as a pet since 1972, may give that animal away to another person or to an animal sanctuary, as long as the ape is not used for commercial purposes by the new owner." "Overview of Great Apes under the Endangered Species Act," Animal Legal and Historical Center, Michigan State University, https://www.animallaw.info.

Merrills and their animal park in Lisbon Falls, including photos of a couple of their monkeys.[37] Next was the astonishing information from Lynne Holland that there had in fact been a second animal park in the area during that time: the Simpson Animal Park in Brunswick, on Old Bath Road, run by Alice E. Simpson.

This really made me scratch my head. There was not just one exotic animal refuge in the immediate area, but two? What a wild environment to have around you as you were growing up. The Durham/Brunswick area had multiple locations harboring wide varieties of unusual animal life nestled in the rural Maine countryside of the 1970s. This was a very different image of the area than I had in my imagination.

After pondering this, I finally sat down and pressed the send button on an email to the last remaining eyewitness of the Durham gorilla. It was a roll of the dice, but through a typically random small world chain of connections, it all came together. Tammy Sairo did not exist any more—never had, in fact. Her real name had been misspelled over and over again. However, properly spelled Tammy Sairio didn't exist anymore either. Instead, it was Tamara Saarinen who I emailed.

When I talked to her in person many weeks later, she admitted that she had opened my email, read it and then closed it again. Eventually, she decided to respond. Why take a chance with me? It was my last name. Tamara works at the University of Maine. My mother worked there for many years before retiring, and for a brief moment in time, I did too. While Tamara did not know me or my mother, she knew *of* us, and she took a gamble, hoping I was the right person to work with her on telling her experience of seeing what became known as the Durham Gorilla. I still feel very lucky and grateful that she decided to hit reply that evening.

We chatted back and forth before our eventual meeting. I learned a few of her sore spots, including the idea that the creature was nothing more than an escaped ape. Tamara shared my view that we don't know everything about the world around us, and we have to keep asking questions to find out more. By mid-May 2019, it was time for our field trip. I had worried it would never actually happen. When I arrange to meet a witness, there is nothing stopping them from changing their mind and deciding they don't want to talk to me after all. I can take nothing for granted. But it worked out great.

The weather was gray but not rainy, the local trees still not leafed out.[*] We sat in her vehicle, talking about her experience and looking at a sketch she had done for me that approximated what she had seen, although she

---

[*] May 2019 ran about two weeks behind southern Maine's usual leafing-out schedule.

confessed her sketching skills were out of practice. We drove to a location she knew well but had not seen in many years. The approach we took was different than I would have taken on my own, because Tamara wanted to show me how she would have biked that summer and the landmarks that had been her daily map, pedaling between Brunswick and Durham.

We drove past her childhood home, past the Huntingtons' home and along the Shiloh Road, which turns into Lisbon Road, where we stopped. Tamara explained that the homes and sidestreets across from us were not there in 1973; in fact, from the site all the way back to Graham Road, there hadn't been much of anything but woods and an occasional field. The forest here was a typical Maine mix of evergreen and deciduous trees, which by July, would form a verdant awning, closing in an arch over the narrow road. As Tamara described, "Riding through this whole area was like riding through this green, lush canopy. Which is why we liked to do it. It was a great place to ride."

There was little traffic on the road. Tamara swears that in 1973 "I could have stood there for hours and there wouldn't have been a car."* The kids biked these roads all summer long, going place to place. It was the time before bike helmets, and the kids would ride in the middle of the lane, rather than the unpredictable mix of gravel and sand forming the narrow verge.

It was midday on June 25, 1973. Twelve-year-old Tammy had slept over at Lois's house the night before. They were good friends, even though Lois was almost a year older than her. Unfortunately, today they had Lois's little brothers, George Jr. and Scott, tagging along on their smaller bikes, and Lois had to slow down for them. Tammy couldn't help zooming ahead, enjoying the air swooshing past her face as she pedaled along.

She realized as she got to the crest of the hill past Jones Cemetery that the others were way behind. She couldn't even see them, although it was so quiet in the bright sunlight that it was still easy to hear them hollering as they biked closer. They were all the way back around the bend in Shiloh Road, about a quarter mile away. She looked into the woods to her right as she waited, and suddenly, nothing else mattered.

---

* Even during our May 2019 visit, Tamara spent a good amount of time standing in the middle of the road with impunity, making me nervous since I'm used to higher-traffic Portland, but to my amazement, we saw only a few vehicles (and one jogger) go by during our forty-minute visit.

Staring back out at her from the dim shadows of the forest, about thirty or forty feet from where she stood with her bike in the road, were two piercing yellow-green eyes. The figure was standing in the dim green shadows of the woods, covered in dark fur, which looked black under the shade of the overhanging trees. It was stockier than Tammy and around five feet tall, just a little bit taller than her. It stood upright with well-built shoulders, arms a little longer than her own, a long torso and legs a little shorter than hers proportionately. It stood on two legs behind undergrowth in a gap between trees.

While she was utterly transfixed by its luminous eyes, she noticed the small amount of exposed skin on its face and fingers was dark, its nose flat and its facial hair grew out around its face from the nose, "like it could brush it back with its hands."

The two youngsters from different species stood there and stared at each other, startled and curious, for what felt like forever but was probably only about five minutes. Then Lois and her brothers—who Tammy had completely forgotten about—arrived, and chaos erupted. Seeing what Tammy was staring at, Lois let out a scream, skidding to a stop and falling off her bike.

The creature broke eye contact with Tammy. Knowing it couldn't stay there with someone shrieking like that but still fascinated, it hesitated and then pivoted and departed swiftly on two feet, vanishing into the shadowy woods.

In a jumble, the kids collected themselves and headed home, since Lois's scraped knee needed attending to. Of course, why the spill happened was blurted out, and the Huntingtons called Blaine Footman, the local deputy sheriff. Shortly after Footman showed up to take their report, Tammy's father whisked her home away from the chaotic scene, with little idea of how much more uproar was in store. Her parents kept her away from the area, although she admits after the furor died down she went back to the location a number of times. "I mean, there was never any sense to it because I never saw anything." But she felt like she had to look anyway.

TAMARA RECALLS BEING CONCERNED about how the press presented the incident. She hadn't felt in danger. "It wasn't scary; it was just weird." The creature was just another curious kid, staring back at her, each trying to figure out what the heck the other one was. Tamara remembers being angry that Lois had scared it away. "And I was really, really angry that they started the circus. And the circus was *serious*."

Whatever the creature was, it didn't stick around once the beer-drinking, gun-toting masses descended on the area with their loud announcements about protecting the town from this dangerous creature. Looking at the results of the media furor, she refers to it as nothing less than a "witch hunt" and a "twenty-seven ring circus."

In the following days, her father made sure that if any evidence emerged, Tamara had an opportunity to see it. Conversely, Tamara definitely doesn't recall being shown the photo of the gorilla costume that police say they displayed to eyewitnesses. Her family never doubted her. They had always taken her seriously, even as a child. Her father shared her desire to learn more about what she had seen. He already thought she was special, so "of course it picked you!"

When Jean and Peter Merrill found a footprint at the back of Jones Cemetery around 7:30 p.m. on Friday, July 27,[38] Tammy's dad took her to see the footprint cast. Off duty, Deputy Sheriff Paul LaFrance was with the Merrills while it was cast, having been in the area at the time. The print was taken to Blaine Footman's home (which also served as his office), where he documented the cast by taking photos of it. Peter Merrill planned to keep the cast, which he thought looked like a chimpanzee track, to pursue further identification.

Deputy Sheriff Blaine Footman described it: "It's about five inches wide with the thumb part broken off. Whatever made it weighs 300 or 350 pounds, and I can't tell you much more. It's definitely not a bear track. I don't know what's going on here, and I'd rather not express an opinion."[39] The track was reported as "rather deep," and Tamara does recall that "it looked like something had hit the ground hard, and the ground had given." The Durham town line side of the Jones Cemetery slopes off to a boggy wooded area, now partially cleared for development, and the back end of the cemetery slopes down into a series of forested gullies and ridges. Both areas have soft, damp soil that would receive a footprint clearly.*

The most interesting thing I figured out from our site visit was that Tamara's sighting of the so-called Durham Gorilla did not occur in Durham at all; it happened on the Brunswick side of the town line, which is now clearly posted, although the sign appears brand new.

---

* Tamara recalls during the exploration of the nearby woods that the search team found a burned-out car, old and abandoned out of sight, far behind the cemetery. The wire fence that circles the cemetery today, she thinks, was added sometime later and wasn't there at the time of the incident.

Jones Cemetery in Brunswick, near Durham town line. *Photo by Michelle Y. Souliere.*

She thinks the creature she met was not an adult: "I didn't think we were much different in age, honestly. And that was the tragedy for me. Because I felt like they were chasing a child. And where was its mother? And where was its home?"

The story of the missing gorilla costume from Drapeau's Costume Shop that ended the story's news cycle with artificially neat finality bothers her. "I tried desperately to believe that it was someone in a suit. I tried desperately to make sense of 'It was an escaped ape.' And it doesn't make any sense to me. It's not what I remember. I mean, it's a horrible drawing [referring to the sketch she made for me], but it's very clear to me, in my head. The head was round. [Its hair] was very black, but the woods were very dark, so I don't know if in the sunlight it would have been as black. The whole face was covered [or dark] except for these two eyes, which were just frankly kind of mesmerizing.

"I have wanted to believe any of these explanations. Because it doesn't make any sense." Tamara works with data all day at her job. Question marks like this bother her—it means data is missing. Public theory about the event does not fit what she saw. But what did she see? She is left believing "very definitely that we don't know everything," a sensible, open-ended observation.

Her greatest regret is that "whatever chance we had to make contact, we blew it completely out of the water" because of the local response at the time. "The woods got invaded....They were going to kill this thing, because it was a threat to the community. I didn't feel a threat. I didn't say 'a threat.' And I never forgave Lois for screaming, honestly." If she could do it all over again, she says, "I wouldn't have told anybody. If I had had the choice, if I had been alone. I might have told my dad. But I would not have told anyone else. And if I saw it now, I don't believe I would ever tell anyone."

In the next couple of years after the event, she and Lois started high school. Everything changed after that summer, and they lost track of each other. Tammy eventually went to Brunswick High, riding her bike the six to eight miles there (depending on her route) until she got her car license. Life went on, as it does, and had its ups and some serious downs, but like most of us, Tamara pushed through and made it out the other side.

In years since, flare-ups of interest in the story have continued. In 2014, *Survivor* star Bob Crowley got *Bangor Daily News* reporter Seth Koenig to write about the topic in a roundabout fashion in relation to Crowley's newly opened 105-acre yurt campground in Durham. Nearby Runaround Pond had recently seen an uncanny number of "large animal carcasses being discarded on the ice."[40] One Star Wars tauntaun carcass photo-op joke on Facebook later, Koenig was surprised to find out that Crowley had been contacted by local Bigfoot hunter Bill Brock, who wanted the carcasses as bait for camera traps.

In April 2015, the crew of *Finding Bigfoot* almost certainly talked to George Huntington's family, if wife Sandi's recollection of "the TV show, *Bigfoot Watchers* or whatever" means what I think it does. A good chunk of the crew's time was spent in the Durham/Brunswick area, as well as neighboring Pownal, and they interviewed Brunswick local investigator Dan Soucy, although this was cut before airing.

In 2016, Bill Brock, Durham resident and Bigfoot hunter, appeared in both a *Down East* magazine article about Durham[41] and a *Times Record* article about the Durham Gorilla. The *Down East* article is an interesting read and focuses on Durham's own particular strangeness. In the *Times Record* article, Brock pressed his theory the "gorilla" is really a Sasquatch.[42]

In other words, media attention has returned again and again to this case, usually without adding any new details and often adding misinformation.

Tamara standing at the site of her encounter. *Photo by Michelle Y. Souliere.*

Every Durham person I talked to expressed frustration and disgust with the media's superficial treatment of their history. I'd like to think that I am able to give you a wider view of the Durham of that time, but I am well aware that even adding what I can, those bits are tiny facets of a much larger, layered and complex picture that only the people who lived there at the time can truly explain. I aim to do my best to add to readers' understanding of this story's context and hope I don't create more confusion in the process.

It is difficult to talk about Durham without also talking about its neighbor Brunswick. Brunswick and Durham share a border, with Durham sitting to the northwest of coastal Brunswick. Both are bordered to the north by the Androscoggin River. They are closely joined but maintain major differences. Durham is in Androscoggin County, while Brunswick is in Cumberland County. Durham's population is sparse, about one-fifth of Brunswick's, give or take.* In 1973, Durham had only 1,264 residents. That's about 32 people per square mile, increasing to about 103 people per square mile in 2010. Durham is also the historic home of fiercely independent religious groups, including the Kingdom/Shilohites and the Quakers. Both remain substantial Durham landowners.

Among the factors dragged into the fray of speculative reporting during the original Durham Gorilla sightings is the existence of Simpson's Animal Park† and Merrill's Wildlife Center. Merrill's was much shorter lived, but circa 1980, it had moved to the Shiloh Road,‡ near where the first Durham Gorilla sighting occurred.

Tamara remembers vaguely another family related to the Merrill's by marriage (the Sears) had a farm on Shiloh Road, where her dad might have

---

* Based on 2010 US Census data, which puts Durham's population at about 3,848 and Brunswick at 20,278.

† Simpson's Animal Park was located at approximately 230 Old Bath Road on the side of Brunswick closer to Bath, separated from the Durham Gorilla activity by both the 295 and US Route 1 corridors. The park opened to the public in 1958. Shortly after owner Frank Simpson's death in 1975, August Lauppe took over the park, continuing to operate it until sometime after 1985. During the decades the park was open, local families were wowed by bears, big cats (including cougars, leopards and lions), monkeys, llamas, donkeys, peacocks and attractions like Frontier Town, a miniature railway on a 1,700-foot-long track circuit, including a fifty-foot tunnel, miniature airplane ride and duck pond with swan boats. On-site performances included jugglers, magic acts and more. A gift shop, snack bar and picnic area complemented the major attractions. Dahlov Ipcar drew inspiration from the animals when seeking life models for her artwork.

‡ Shiloh Road is only about a mile and a half long and does a wacky T-bone thing on its south end, where it extends about six hundred feet before bending and becoming Leighton Road in the west and another six hundred feet before it transforms into Lisbon Road in the east. If there's one thing I've learned about the Durham/Brunswick area, it is that the roads can be surprisingly confusing.

taken her to see ostriches and other exotic birds, about a mile away from the Durham-Brunswick line. But what she described was nothing like what was reported in the 1976 *Maine Times* article,[43] from which my first real information was to be drawn, back when the Merrills were expanding their zoo at their farm in Lisbon.* That, too, was vastly different from the version of Merrill's Wildlife Center that appeared in old photos posted by local fans on the Facebook page of the Durham Historical Society,[44] showing views of the wildlife center circa 1980.

The upshot of this is that while Brunswick and Durham had existing culture that introduced local kids and families to a fascinating array of exotic animal species in the years before and after the Durham Gorilla events, there is not adequate documentation beyond lurid rumor to explain away Tamara's sighting as a runaway monkey or ape. Yes, there were exotic animals, including various smaller primates, living in captivity in the surrounding towns, but out of the species known to be in the area, none matches the description of what she saw in the woods that day.

This incident is a particularly good reminder to keep your eyes open wherever you are.

Note: Dear reader, as you finish with this eyewitness account and move onto the next one, you might be surprised and intrigued to find out that they took place within about three miles of each other.

DURHAM GORILLA ARTICLES IN CHRONOLOGICAL ORDER

Bob Chaffe, "Police Search for 'Monster,'" *Brunswick Times Record*, July 27, 1973, 1, 9.
Portland Press Herald, "Police Hunt Gorilla-Like Beast in Brunswick Area," July 27, 1973, 18.

---

* At the time of the *Maine Times* article, Elaine and Carleton were caring for a wide range of rescued animals on their farm in Lisbon, Maine. These included a Macaque monkey named Rocco, a baby Capuchin monkey named Scotty, another Capuchin named Chico, a squirrel monkey, their lion Ralph (who became the star attraction of their park when they moved to Durham), fallow deer and a coatimundi. The article also mentions the many birds they bred on site for fellow collectors and breeders. Add to that the occasional seal or armadillo, a one-winged crow and an orphaned skunk. Oh, and did we forget all the farm animals and barnyard fowl on site? Even before hitting their full stride, the Merrills had an amazing menagerie. I hope to sit down with Elaine Merrill or her daughter and record more details of Merrill's Wildlife Center someday soon.

Evening Express, "Dog Officer Gets Help in Search for 'Gorilla,'" July 27, 1973, 4.

Lewiston Daily Sun, "Anyone Lose an Ape at Durham?" July 27, 1973, 2.

Richard Brayall, "Lots of Folks Have Seen 'It' but Disagree as to What They Saw," *Lewiston Evening Journal*, July 27, 1973, 2.

Biddeford-Saco Journal, "Gorilla Sightings Reported," July 27, 1973, 1.

Portsmouth Herald, "Dog Officer Hunts Gorilla," July 27, 1973, 2.

Portsmouth Herald, "Beast Hunt Scheduled to Resume," July 27, 1973, 21.

Paul Downing, "'Chimp Theory' Gains Support During Search," *Portland Press Herald*, July 28, 1973, 15.

Evening Express, "Gorillas in Brunswick," July 28, 1973, 8.

Lewiston Daily Sun, "'Monster' Tracks Found in Durham Area; Still Unknown What 'It' Is," July 28, 1973, 2.

Lloyd Ferriss, "Is It a Bear? Phantom? Or a Real Live Chimp?," "Is It Man, Beast, Hoax in Durham?," *Maine Sunday Telegram*, July 29, 1973, 1, 24A.

Bob Chaffee, "Nobody's Found the 'Monster,'" *Brunswick Times Record*, July 30, 1973, 1, back page.

Lewiston Evening Journal, "Durham Monster," July 30, 1973, 4.

Brunswick Times Record, "Still No Sign of the 'Monster,'" July 31, 1973.

Paul Downing, "Police Suspect Hoax in Ape Appearances," *Portland Press Herald*, July 31, 1973, 17. (Not in all editions. On page 6, a purported Bigfoot photo appeared, originating from northeast of Spokane, Washington, showing a figure perched on a cliffside that looks like someone in a gorilla costume.)

Lewiston Daily Sun, "Rented Gorilla Costume Has Not Been Returned," July 31, 1973, 28.

Portsmouth Herald, "Gorilla Suit Reported Stolen," August 1, 1973, 17.

Tamara's eyewitness sketch. *Courtesy of Tamara Saarinen.*

Missing (Based on Loren Coleman's list)

Brunswick Times Record, July 26, 1973. (Library could not find.)

Boston Sunday Globe, July 29, 1973, 27.

Lewiston Daily Sun, July 30, 1973.

7

MIKE LEDBURY

Neighbors out of *National Geographic*

BRUNSWICK, MAINE, CUMBERLAND COUNTY
CIRCA 1975–78

I first found Mike's post, a sentence or two, online in 2011. In 2018, I sent him a message, and he agreed to a phone interview. I was interviewing another person that evening but arranged to call Mike last, since his email mentioned, "This is more than a simple sightings story."

Mike is the first person to ask me more questions up front than I asked him. He wanted to know if I had experienced anything "abnormal." I answered no, but I knew a lot of people who had, and I have a natural curiosity about the unexplained, plus a very open mind. He asked if I was an animal lover. That's easy—anyone who follows me on Instagram knows my two cats. These formalities out of the way, the real talk about his Class A encounters began.

IT IS 1975. MIKE is fifteen years old. Fed up after arguing with his father, he heads outside. He's not going far, just enough to avoid more conflict for tonight. He crosses the road and sets off across the large field facing it. He's heading for a little farm shack set into the edge of the woods—a quiet place where he can build a campfire alone under the stars, where no one will bother him.

In the woods just behind the shed is a ravine. Between the *pop* and *crackle* of his fire, Mike hears noises down there—heavy noises. It's not moose or deer, and his mind jumps at once to the other possibility. Could it be a ticked-off bear? He tries warning it off by yelling, but the noise continues. Suddenly, pieces of wood, rock and other debris pelt his campsite. This doesn't make any sense—what creature would do that? Unnerved, Mike puts out his campfire. He's not willing to head home yet, but he wants to distance himself from these disturbances. He heads for the big hill nearby.

At the top of the hill is a knoll filled with grass about three feet high, perfect to lie in comfortably without being seen. It doesn't take long for Mike to fall asleep. Later, he is woken again. In a cluster of trees about two hundred yards away, it sounds like someone is ripping branches down and tearing them apart. Mike stands up to see over the grass. It's a bright moonlit night, but he can't see what's making all that racket. So, he yells, "Heeeyyyy!" and something inside the tree stand roars back—a roar like he's never heard, until later when he watches a National Geographic special about mountain gorillas.

The next day, he talks to his friend Ben and convinces him to come investigate after school and chores. Walking through the late afternoon sun, Ben carries his shotgun, Mike a borrowed .22. They start at the grassy knoll, then track over to the stand of alders. They examine the trees. Branches have been torn from the trees at a level which even Ben, over six feet tall, can't reach. Something ripped the branches down, shredded them and made a pile of leaves in the glade. Both boys are perplexed.

They head to the shack. Dusk is falling as they hear a noise from below in the ravine. Once again, a full-throated roar erupts from the shadows, and debris is launched at them from the woods. They yell, "What are you doing? Get out of here!" at what they think might be some troublemaker messing with them. The roaring continues, and Ben lets fly a shotgun round into the overhead foliage as a warning. Sounds of rapid retreat are heard, but they don't give chase; they've had enough. They run home pell-mell across the field, asking each other breathlessly, "What *is* that thing? WHAT IS IT?"

Later, Mike goes for a weekend hike. Maine in autumn will take your mind off most things, and it's a particularly nice day. He follows a game trail, which ends at a bit of a cliff, dropping about sixty feet down to a streambed ravine. There is a lone pine tree next to the stream. Looking at the tree, he realizes something is looking back at him. It looks about eight feet tall and is unmistakably covered in fur. Standing there with his mouth hanging open, Mike searches his mind for all the large mammals he knows from the area, but nothing he's ever seen compares to this—not a bear or a moose or anything else. Whatever it is, it stands right there and stares back.

A typical ridge and gully in the woods near Mike's childhood home. It is difficult to convey the drama of this landscape in a photo. *Photo by Michelle Y. Souliere.*

There's nothing left to do but freak out. Mike turns around. He runs. He runs for home.

His mind goes in circles. It looked like an ape. Some big giant ape standing around. His mind reels and latches onto a local story from a couple years before—could it be the Durham Ape? His mind wrestles with this and leaps sideways and lands on the concept of Sasquatch. But here in Maine? That's crazy. No way. What really matters is that it is undeniably some type of primate. He thinks to himself, "This is an ape, and all the stuff I've been reading in *National Geographic* magazine or watching on the National Geographic TV show that my mom has us watch all the time will come in handy." But what to do next?

PART OF ANY GOOD involvement involves talking to locals. Mike and his dad often make the rounds to other farms, picking up various things for repairs or improvements. With his mom running Fireglow Kennels on their property, there are always cats and dogs around, plus a variety of livestock. Between the animals and the crops, there are always things that need fixing and resupplying, like any working farm. Mike gets pretty handy at making inquiries. One throws the net wide. The basic starting point is often, "Did you ever see anything weird?" Most of the time, nothing comes of it.

He and his dad are at a farm in Durham along the woods that border Mike's home in Brunswick on the other side. The farmer seems receptive, and Mike feels encouraged enough this time to add, "You know, I've seen something." He relates his encounters to the man, who agrees he's seen something similar. While out on his tractor in the fields, "I see him, and he's just sitting there. Watching me. So, I'll stop, and I'll smoke my cigarette, and then he'll get up and walk away." It looked like a big giant ape. Furry, kind of brownish, a flattish head. "He just sits there and watches me," he said. Relieved to no longer be alone, Mike nods, adding, "Yup, I've seen the same thing." The farmer hadn't told anyone because most folks would think he's crazy.

Back home, life continues. Mike persuades Ben to go hiking a few more times, but they are followed through the woods constantly. Ben can't take it anymore. Although Mike still goes hunting and hiking with Ben, never again could he convince him to step foot near those particular woods. This just fuels Mike's search. If this is the creature's home, it's *his* home too. And he is curious. He puts his skills to work investigating this mystery.

Mike climbs up the highest ridge and scrambles up its tallest tree. Looking out over the valleys around his perch, he sits and observes. Sometimes he sees clues. "One of the best indicators in the woods, especially in Maine, is the blue jay," he told me. An alert in one of the groves below from these noisy birds lets him know something is going on under the tree cover. He quietly descends from his lookout tree, heading in that direction, listening as he goes. Sometimes he encounters a moose or a bear. Other times, his shadowy neighbor has just been by. He is sure it always knows exactly where he is.

A competitive track runner at school, Mike thinks he can catch his pursuer. One day, he turns and chases the elusive form through the woods, following it uphill, trying to keep pace. After this effort, he decides the only way he will catch it is if it wants him to. This at least rules out a man in a suit. He dons camouflage, only to find, once again, he is the one being followed. It's like it is playing with him.

Mike has no one to talk to besides Ben, who is a good ear but has no interest in joining. His sisters know something is up. He is determined to get to the bottom of the puzzle somehow. He researches the methods used by Dian Fossey and Jane Goodall as they move toward a human-ape understanding. He needs to gain proximity to this mysterious creature. He begins experimenting with different methods. He tries to move through the forest like it does and sits still for long periods of time, watching and listening. He wants to gain its respect and eliminate fear to cultivate familiarity.

In 1977, now around seventeen years old, Mike decides to take a real step forward. He finds a clearing in the woods that looks like a common crossroads for them. Trees are bare, the ground cover looks trampled and a big rock sits smack in the middle of the clearing, an excellent perch. He clears the area, hauling out brush, fallen logs and other debris. With a hatchet and knife, he blazes trees around the clearing, as well as a path in and out of the clearing so that he can find his way even at night. He spends a lot of daytime there. He thinks it won't hurt to mark his territory by peeing on every tree around the edge of the clearing.

He brings fruit with him, oranges and apples mostly, and leaves some behind on the big rock. When the fruit disappears, he doesn't know if it is his unseen neighbor or another forest animal that enjoys the snack, but he hopes it's the more elusive one. He thinks his quarry is more comfortable in the dark. He expands his experiment's parameters once again and ventures out one night.

Moving through the darkening forest, he settles down by the big rock and waits to see what will happen. Eventually, a familiar presence arrives. The big one that he saw in the ravine, and has encountered fleetingly so many times, rattles the trees around the clearing as though to say, "I could do this to you, too," and then starts throwing debris at him. Thinking quickly amid his jangling nerves, Mike drops into a submissive posture, as Dian Fossey did when attempting to gain acceptance from her gorilla neighbors. He crouches down, lowers his head and holds his hands out and down, so the creature can see them clearly.

To his surprise, this works. The big one settles down, crouching too, about fifteen to twenty feet away from Mike on the floor of the clearing. "There he is!" Mike thinks in astonishment. In his hands, he holds fruit, apples and an orange. He tosses them toward the big guy. Suddenly, the forest erupts from behind Mike as they are interrupted by a younger creature, about Mike's size. He is full of challenge, all of a fury in Mike's face—baring his sizeable teeth, howling and screaming at him in a blast, and all Mike can think to do

Tree blazes in the woods near Mike's childhood home (blazed by another party), showing how a too-deep blaze would look after decades of growth. *Photo by Michelle Y. Souliere.*

is take out the knife he has with him; hold it before his face so the creature sees that he has teeth too, big silver teeth; and yell right back at him without backing down.

Things had quickly gone south from their auspicious start. Mike starts thinking about how he's going to get out of there in one piece. He can see other forms moving in the undergrowth around the clearing at the edge of his vision.

Coaching himself over and over again not to turn and run, he backs away step by step until he reaches the tree line. Just then a hand comes down on his shoulder from behind. Returning to this moment decades later, Mike loops his speech: "I'm freaking out. I'm freaking out." He thinks this peripheral member of the group might be a female because of the difference in approach but sees only enough to tell that the creature is smaller than the big one and bigger than the small one. He almost breaks and runs but knows "that would have been *bad*." He ducks beneath the hand and continues his retreat, backing up until he spots his trail blaze in the dark, and then he gets out of there.

"You might think I was crazy or something," he says now, "but I had to see it through. Thinking about it now, that was pretty crazy." A combat veteran from Desert Storm, with twenty years of military experience before retiring to a civilian career, Mike admits he has an affinity for adrenaline. Nowadays, though, he prefers situations where he has assessed the risk: "I try to do controlled scary things." In addition to spending time in the wild when he can, he surfs. But after that dark night in those woods, he was done with risk-taking for a while.

From then on, he and the creatures coexisted, aware of one another's nearness. "Once I had the encounter, I was good to go. I kind of got it out of my system," he says. "I knew he was out there, and I just…kind of left him alone." It was as though the knowledge that an introduction had been made was enough. Things returned to normal. As Mike said to me, "It's just an animal. It's not some mythical being. It's just real good at hiding." Quiet and observant, they are the "world champion of hide-and-seek."

I asked if he'd seen evidence of what foods they ate besides fruit. He'd never caught any of them by surprise while they were eating but had noticed one thing. "I think they used tools. You'd find a grouse head, and you'd find a bloody stick with grouse feathers on it. And I'm thinking, hmm. I like grouse, and maybe they do too." There were abundant crops, including large cornfields, nearby, plus apple orchards, cattails, blueberry fields and blackberry patches, and a plethora of wildlife—game birds, beaver, muskrat, minks, martins, bobcats, moose, bear, deer and more. "It was a phenomenal place to grow up. I had all these animals. And then I found that Bigfoot, and I was like wow! To me, that was Disney World."

Mike returned to Maine recently to climb Mouth Katahdin with his sons, stopping to show them where he used to live. He hasn't spent time in Maine since joining the navy in 1978 straight out of high school. The house he grew up in is long gone, a victim of Androscoggin floods. I asked if he went into the woods with his sons. He said no, "not those woods." He showed them where the house had been and told them a little bit about his encounter. They buy him Bigfoot T-shirts and birthday cards and joke with him about it.

He never found any Bigfoot lairs, though he searched. He would find other creatures' dens where fallen trees had been hollowed out underneath. He is still curious about the caverns and crevices he spotted in the ravine areas, but he never tried to venture deep into those overgrown areas and sections too swampy to navigate. But in truth, Mike says, "The only time I ever saw them was up in the higher areas and the game trails where I was."

He didn't take a camera with him into the woods. His quarry was on the move when he was around and so quick that getting a camera out in time seemed futile. I asked him if he'd thought of taking a camera with him during the encounter in his clearing that night, and he said, "I could have taken pictures, but I was afraid. I would not have dared having a camera at night, with a flash. I don't know what that would have done. No."

He experimented with carrying firearms visibly, as he did with other behavioral triggers over the years. If he went into the woods carrying a gun, they tended to not show up. He thinks they visually recognize guns and might be able to smell the gun oil. When he first started looking for them, he had to go in clean. "I had to be real careful of how I smelled" or else they would stay away. Eventually, this didn't matter as much. He thinks they became more curious as time went on. But he had little luck drawing them out if he brought company with him.

He described their coats as brownish, "a mottled brown with some black in it," thick and shaggy, hiding their ears from view. Beyond the hairless areas on the soles of their feet, the palms of their hands and small sections of their faces, the rest of their bodies were entirely covered in hair. The torso and the head were shaggier. "There's a lot [of hair] on the head on the top and around the brow. The neck is covered pretty good, what little neck they do have." Around the eyes and on the exposed part of their cheeks, he describes heavily pigmented skin: "A thick darkish skin…like gorillas have."

Their hands and feet are large, as they themselves are altogether large and muscular. The big one he describes as between seven and eight feet tall, and the one that laid its hand on his shoulder in the dark was over six feet tall and slender. The younger one he estimates at about five foot eleven, around Mike's own height at the time. While Mike was about 155 pounds, he recalls the youngster had "a bit more weight on him." They show good muscular tone under their fur. Their eyes are dark, large "and very intelligent-looking." He estimates their eyes look larger than most great apes. While he doesn't think they are as smart as *Homo sapiens*, he thinks they are a lot more developed than most apes, which allows them to outwit people in the woods time and time again. He refutes the claims that they stink. He describes it more as a "gamey smell," like the normal smell of any wild animal or a wet horse, for instance.

Their posture is upright, unless stalking something or trying to be very quiet. At these times, he has seen them on all fours, creeping through the undergrowth low to the ground. He didn't encounter them much during the winter, but when out snowshoeing, "every once in a while, I'd see big footprints where they were going through....It would be like he was stove-piping through all this deep snow....Something had been through there. You could see it was only two-legged." He opted not to actively search out their winter lair. "It was probably some deep crevice somewhere, in a cave or something. But I didn't want to go bother them. That probably would have been pushing it, if I found their lair in the wintertime."

Although anchored to the nearby area, they had nomadic tendencies, sometimes disappearing for periods of time. He thought they might move off to parts of the forest he wasn't getting into himself.

The sounds he heard, beyond territorial roars and howls, included occasional wood-knocking "way off in the woods." He puzzled over it later. He heard them whistle while out stalking. "Hard to believe, but they can whistle like a bird." Even more interesting, he believes he made one laugh once:

I was down in one of the ravines, down in the stream area, and I noticed there was a deer down in there, so I go into stalk mode. I crept down in there. It's taking me forever. Now when you're moving, you're moving when the wind blows. You just inch your way, inch your way, inch your way. I'm low crawling towards this deer. I crawl through the bushes. There's certain techniques to crawl through here [so] you don't make the bushes move or make noise or anything like that.

So, I get ten, probably eight feet behind this female deer. It doesn't even know I'm there. I'm thinking, I can't get any closer, because if I spook her, she'll kick me. But then I kind of raise up on my haunches, and I go, "ʙᴏᴏ!" That scared it, and it was kind of like a cartoon. It jumped straight up in the air and then it ran off. And when I did that, I heard something in the woods, in the bushes a little farther away from me, go, "Heh-heh-heh."

Now when I was in the woods, I always knew they followed me around. And sometimes I see them, and sometimes I don't. To me, it sounded like this creature laughed at me....He got the biggest kick out of me spooking that deer. He was sitting there watching me, probably wondering what I was going to do, and then I scared it. I didn't even know [the big guy] *was there. It was probably about 150, 200 feet away from me, up in the woods, just watching the whole thing, you know?*

Mike reiterated that the approach Dian Fossey and Jane Goodall used was the only way to get close to these creatures and build anything like a rapport with them. "You can't just chase these things. You've got to get them to respect you and trust you." He thinks most people will encounter them only by accident, otherwise.

He laments that his real hope has yet to come true. After confirming his experience to his own satisfaction but figuring no one else would believe him, he waited patiently through military and civilian careers, through a marriage and three kids. As a kid, he'd thought, "One day, somebody's going to go out there, and they're going to prove to the world that there is Bigfoot." An adult with a position in the scientific community would come forward with information similar to his own and the proof demanded by their peers. As he says now, "I've been waiting forty-three years for someone to come forward and say that there's Bigfoot out there. I don't know why they haven't found it....Now it's forty-three years later, and they still call it a myth."

But honestly, he knows *exactly* why. He remarked on the techniques that are in common use right now—the crowds of people on publicized expeditions descending en masse on their wooded area of choice, the lights, the blaring recorded calls on huge speakers, everyone dressed like hunters. As he puts it succinctly, "If Bigfoot was anywhere there, he's now fifty miles away."

I think even today, he doesn't expect anyone to believe him. The few people he's told have either ignored him or made light of it. "They don't know what to think about it because *they've* never encountered it, you know? And that's my own family." He chuckles, amused a little himself. I think he's surprised I actually called him and wanted to hear it all for myself. But I, too, grew up

A Brunswick powerline corridor in winter. A great place to track animal activity after fresh snow has fallen. *Photo by Michelle Y. Souliere.*

reading every issue of *National Geographic* and watched the weekly television specials with my family. My dad, a biology and field science teacher at a local high school, had book after book about the natural world, and I pored over them for hours throughout my childhood. It was a near miss that I went into the arts instead of biology. Mike himself admitted his dream as a kid was to train as a zoologist. But as he said, "that didn't happen."

Life is a funny thing, full of surprises with no explanation sometimes. It's what keeps it interesting. Don't you agree?

8

JANELLE GRAF

A Family History of Encounters

Skowhegan Area, Somerset County
Summer 1977 to Present

I thought I'd lost my chance with this case, but sometimes the world being small works out. In February 2008, Janelle Graf posted online about her father's 1970s sighting (and her own). Unfortunately, her listed email was defunct. In late 2018, I realized she was in an online Bigfoot group I frequented. I wasted no time getting in touch this time around. Janelle's case is especially interesting because it is a collective encounter. She and her father were not alone—many relatives and neighbors encountered something inexplicable. Some of these Somerset County encounters are Class A sightings, though unfortunately, many of the eyewitnesses are now gone, including Fred Moody himself.

It was the spring of 1977, the year of Janelle's tenth birthday. Outside, the night yawned pitch black when her dad, Fred Moody, woke her up, urgently telling her to follow him outdoors. Flashlights in hand, they ran to the end of their house, looking down over the field toward the barn. She was horrified by the sounds coming from inside. Their pig's squeals were punctuated by the sound of something being thrashed against the walls inside.

As they stopped in the gap between the house and the garage, there was no time to think. Her dad, holding his gun, told Janelle to aim the flashlight at the barn door. She did. His gun followed the light of the beam through

A map of the Skowhegan/Cornville/Canaan region. Maine General Highway Atlas, *1959*.

the dark as he yelled, "Get out of there!" Bursting through the door on its hind legs, something tall and covered in brown hair came running out and sprinted across the field into the woods. Her dad ran after it, firing a couple of times as Janelle struggled to keep up with the flashlight. It was gone.

The next morning, Janelle's dad yelled from the barn. They were greeted by a grisly mess. The pig lay dead, badly mutilated in the struggle the night before. The walls and ceiling were splashed in blood. It looked like the pig had been picked up and thrown against the wall repeatedly. At first, they assumed what had run out of the barn was a bear, but it never went down on all fours. Later her dad told Janelle that he believed it was something else entirely, something that wasn't supposed to exist. By then, he had seen it again.

In June 1977, Janelle's dad was cutting timber on the big ridge behind their home. An avid hunter, trapper and fisherman, his CB handle was the Careful Poacher. He made his living as a logger, often working alongside his brothers, and owned his own skidder and pulp truck. Janelle was used to her dad not being afraid of anything. That day he ran down the field toward the house, thrashing the door when he found it locked. Janelle moved quickly to let him in, alarmed. He pushed through the doorway, jamming it shut again as he gasped to her, "Lock the door! It's chasing me!" He was white as a ghost as he grabbed his gun, going to the window to watch the tree line.

He had been on the skidder working when something started throwing rocks at him. He looked around, thinking it was one of his brothers. Instead, he saw something like a man but covered in long dark hair all over its body. Standing seven to eight feet tall, it circled his skidder about seventeen yards away. Janelle's dad shut off the skidder. The creature stopped. It watched him. He yelled at it to get out of there, and it started screeching at him unlike anything he'd heard before. The creature continued throwing boulders at him, so he got down off the skidder, leaving it between him and his aggressor. He headed home, trying not to run and escalate its pursuit. The creature was soon out of sight, and he thought it was gone.

Then the screams started again. It wasn't gone; it was keeping pace with him down the slope, staying about twenty yards away. He could hear it crashing through bushes, breaking and knocking down trees, blasting scream after scream at him. He could smell it, too, as he caught glimpses of it through the trees. As he emerged from the tree line into the field, he finally gave into the need to run without looking back.

Safe inside, he watched through the back window. Then he rang up his brothers. Later arriving with rifles, the men went back up the slope together. They found broken trees and tracks left in the creature's wake, but the beast was gone. The skidder had big dents in its metal top panels from where hefty rocks had hit it during the attack. After the incident, Janelle's dad called the sheriff. Maine game wardens came to take his statement. A newspaper story about the account appeared in the *Somerset Reporter* on June 23, 1977, mostly correct.

Later that summer, going out to the garden to do her weeding chores, Janelle found bare footprints in the soft earth. Something had walked into the garden and back out again. The tracks were very large, and some plants had been pulled up. Janelle's dad called back the game warden who was taking the case seriously because he knew Fred Moody was an experienced woodsman who wouldn't lie about such serious incidents. Janelle remembers the game warden took footprint casts and photos. She remembers other officials seemed to think her dad was making it all up, as did some of the reporters.

Over the next few weeks, as Janelle's dad and uncles worked in the woods, the creature was out there, too, stalking them. Janelle and her siblings were forbidden to go into the woods at all. Her dad started carrying both his .303 British rifle and his camera, but the creature didn't show itself to him again.

Janelle had always tagged along with her dad when he trapped and fished and played around the forest by herself. It was easy to forget she'd been warned to stay away. One warm sunny day, not long after she found the mysterious footprints, some cousins came to visit. They played near the garden in the open field but quickly tired of baking like hot potatoes in the sun. Just inside the tree line was a shady clearing where they set up house during visits, calling it their cabin. It didn't seem like it would cause any harm, because what could happen only ten feet into the woods? They were glad to be playing in the cooler shade but started noticing a nasty, rank odor. Suddenly, Janelle remembered her dad mentioning the bad smell encountered while fleeing the creature. It was acrid like rotting meat or something that was dead. Janelle could feel it burning the inside of her nose.

She got everyone out of the clearing and sent them toward the house but realized she'd left something behind. She ran back, bending down to pick up her belonging, and was terrified to hear a noise behind her. She stood and turned. It was there, standing no more than ten feet from her. It was very still, looking at her. She screamed, and it gave a grunt. Janelle ran and didn't look back. She never returned to their cabin hideout again.

At this time, she was about four feet tall and thought the creature was about double that. The creature's hair was about three to five inches long and dark with a mixture of gray, red and light brown streaks. When she saw the movie *Harry and the Hendersons* years later, she felt a shock of recognition looking at the color of Harry's coat. The skin on the face of the creature was pigmented like a dark tan (again, using Harry as a point of comparison, a little darker than his), with a prominent eyebrow ridge casting a shadow over its eyes. The Patterson-Gimlin footage is the closest she has seen to the creature's proportions.

That summer, sightings trickled in from relatives and neighbors. Janelle's eighty-year-old uncle and his wife were coming to visit her family when they saw something in a field full of tall weeds and dandelions half a mile south of Janelle's home. Her uncle said the creature was pulling dandelions and shoving them into its mouth, a seemingly harmless occupation, but the sight so shattered him that Janelle's aunt took him to the emergency room, thinking he was having a heart attack. He had gone stark white and couldn't speak for a good ten minutes, mute with shock. Janelle's aunt took Janelle's dad to the location and found "a big round area that had been all flattened out like it had been lying there in the grass."

Around the same time, a woman who lived a few miles south of Janelle's home came by. She had been hanging laundry in her yard and watched two Bigfoots, one large and one small (maybe an adult female and a young one), walk across her backyard and cross the nearby road, heading south. Nearby, on a different road a couple of miles from Janelle's home, Janelle's father and two friends headed out to check their traps. Just before their trapping site, a large Bigfoot stood in the middle of the road urinating. It ran off into the woods when it saw them.

After seeing how Janelle's dad had been treated, eyewitnesses came to the Moodys to talk about what they had seen instead of going to the authorities. But the sightings have continued, whether talked about publicly or not. Today Janelle continues to advocate for the public to treat eyewitnesses with courtesy and respect and follows in her father's footsteps, collecting accounts from locals who trust her enough to share their own experiences.

Around 2002, Janelle found herself back in the deep end of Bigfoot sightings when one morning her college-age son arrived home with a friend in tow. The night before, a friend had thrown a post-graduation party at his family's camp. The camp was set high above a half-mile-wide gully that was boggy-bottomed and filled with undergrowth, its deepest part showing as a silver ribbon down the center of its length.

On the other side of this stream, just visible from the small lawn was an old sign tacked several feet above the water on a dead tree, useful for long-distance target practice. That night, they readied by turning on a spotlight and aiming it at the sign. They were shocked to see eyes flaring red back at them as they swung the light across. Something was walking through the deepest boggy area. The creature stood upright. Its lower body, part of its hands included, was below the surface of the water, usually four or five feet deep in that area. Janelle's son estimated its head

Looking down from the camp over the boggy valley area the creature waded through near Skowhegan. *Photo by Michelle Y. Souliere.*

and torso towered another four feet above the water, making its total height around eight feet. It looked up at the light two or three times as it walked away, its eyes flashing red before it disappeared into the dark night. The small group of friends retreated into the camp house, where they stayed until morning. This camp is close to where Janelle and her dad had their encounters.

A few years later, shortly after Thanksgiving 2005, Janelle, her eldest daughter and her son-in-law were in a clear-cut seeking a good Christmas tree when wood knocks rang out and rocks were thrown at them from a nearby ridge. This behavior was apparently triggered when they hammered a tree to remove something nailed to it. At first it was funny, and they kept knocking on the tree, getting return knocks every time. But when the noises turned to the loud *thump* impact of boulders being lobbed in their direction from the woods, it was clearly time for them to leave quickly.

In 2006, her daughter had an encounter of her own while heading home with friends one night, when a similar creature crossed the road ahead of them, striding down the bank into yet another boggy area.

Janelle tried to report her family's encounters, but it wasn't until 2007 that the BFRO finally sent a representative to interview her, which Janelle described as a letdown. The young man "spent his time…trying to find someone who would talk to him about current sightings," and when that failed, he went off to the logging roads to look for fresh tracks. The problem was, he came during the winter, when sites were snowed in, and got his vehicle stuck on a restricted trail (since he drove instead of hiking in), a violation that is fined heavily.

Janelle states that the BFRO continued to dismiss her family's sightings because her uncles had passed away and her father now had Alzheimer's and could not be interviewed—ignoring her statements about her own encounters. When she showed them the 1977 press clippings, they belatedly showed interest again, but she was fed up with them.

This mixed response to her family's encounters was nothing new. In 1977, she remembers, game wardens took casts and photos of the prints in their garden, but those pieces of evidence met a murky fate. Janelle states that as an adult she worked alongside the responding warden, and he told her any existing footprint casts and photos were destroyed.

When I talked to former game warden James Ross in March 2019 via telephone shortly before his retirement, he was chief deputy sheriff of Somerset County. He didn't recall having access to plaster casting material or camera equipment* as a game warden but made one thing very clear: Janelle's dad, Fred Moody, "was a very experienced woodsman…very woods-savvy." He had no doubt Moody had been badly scared by something and that he was not someone who would misidentify a black bear, common in the Skowhegan area at that time.

When Ross was dispatched to the Moodys' after the skidder incident, he found Fred "obviously shaken, and when we went back down into the area, I recall finding tracks where he said it had run off to. In a large anthill was in fact a very large footprint, *very* large." The footprint was "much, much bigger than any human being would ever make, much larger than a bear would make. So, I believe he thinks he saw a Bigfoot."

---

* Chief Deputy Ross was careful with what he said, as any good law enforcement officer would be. He knew I was recording our phone conversation for the purpose of double-checking my notes. He specifically mentioned the dearth of plaster-casting and photos on his own after I asked how wardens documented cases of problematic large mammals at the time. He was friendly and courteous and open about his experiences. He regularly reminded me how long ago they had occurred and that he didn't remember everything. For instance, he didn't remember returning to the Moodys' for the tracks in the garden.

He told me, "I've always been convinced that somebody was playing tricks on him. I think that the track that we saw was probably staged there. But he believed what he saw, I'm convinced of that."*

THE WORLD OF A 1970s Maine game warden was very different from today. Ross was only three or four months into his long career in 1977. Wardens worked alone most of the time, and Ross was responsible for a half dozen towns east of the Kennebec River, from Solon down to Skowhegan. Duties included dealing with problems that are rarer today, due to laws put in place over the intervening years. For instance, the problem of deer mortality from domestic dogs was a major issue then.†

"You were on twenty-four-hour call, so you were expected to handle all your complaints and activity during the day, but you were also expected to be out there at night." Ross estimates, "There were many, many weeks where the average game warden was working well over 100 hours a week. Some weeks it might be 120 hours. And you were paid for your 40 [hours], there was no overtime, there was no comp time. You worked it." Ross thinks that "what made the job so fascinating and interesting, is that every day was totally different, and you never knew what was going to happen from minute to minute." From missing children and hunters to waiting in the dark for poachers, a warden's work was never done, but it was never boring, either. "When you went to the end of your driveway, most days, it was whether you turned left or right." And where you started out could be far from where you ended your day.

Ross worked in the Skowhegan area for about thirteen and a half years before being promoted to sergeant and transferring to southern Maine, after which he shifted every few years for a total of over twenty-two years in the warden service. After finding himself an administrator, far from what he

---

* Chief Deputy Ross clearly had great respect for Fred Moody. In fact, he did not mention him by name until after I had, in the same way that Janelle didn't mention Ross by name until after I researched and found the information myself. This demonstrates the great respect for privacy and care in not involving others by name until good intent and effort are verified in the Skowhegan area community. Janelle didn't talk to me in detail until after contacting a mutual friend and verifying that I wasn't associated with troublemakers. Just as I double-check interviewee information, so did many of them double-check my bona fides as well.

† Ross recalled, "In the spring, this time of year [March], we used to get very bad dog/deer problems that we had to deal with, very heavy mortality on the deer herd. That's changed now with the leash laws. There's nowhere near the problem of dogs at large getting into the deer." Maine's regulation of unleashed/uncontrolled dogs, that is "dogs at large," was finally addressed in legislation in 1987. Maine Legislature, https://www.mainelegislature.org/legis/statutes/7/title7sec3911.html.

wanted out of life, he retired to employ his hard-earned skills elsewhere. If Ross experienced grief from his peers and superiors for standing up on behalf of Fred Moody, he did not mention it to me, although Janelle remembered Ross telling her that things hadn't been easy in the wake of summer 1977.

If former warden Ross and Janelle's accounts differ on some details, what remains rock solid is this: Janelle's dad, Fred Moody, was a man to be believed, even when he said he'd seen an unbelievable thing.

Let's delve into some newspaper clippings. Janelle was given a copy of both known articles by James Ross and is sure that more exist buried in archives. One article is from the *Somerset Reporter*,[45] which asks, "Is something out there?" It tells of a creature reported by woodsmen in the Skowhegan area and two nighttime roadside sightings. This article was about three times longer than the *Bangor Daily News* article, which preceded it by several days.

The *Somerset Reporter* article describes the creature as roughly seven feet tall, covered in hair "finer than a bear or a deer" and walking upright. The game warden states that the footprints show four toes and measure about eighteen inches long but had not been cast, explaining, "With this rain it's been hard to get back into the woods" with casting material. The witness, Fred Moody, stated, "I didn't get to see its face, but I got a good look at it side-to. It had a flat face, with no nose or ears that I could see. And it had hands, just like the hands that we've got."[*]

The warden supervisor, Larry Cummings, vouched for the witness in the article, calling him "completely trustworthy," stating, "If he says he saw something, I'm certain that he did. What it is, I wouldn't venture to guess." Lamenting, "If we could get a picture, or a track, or anything, then I'd feel a lot better," Moody closed the article saying, "I'll say this, though, I'm carrying a camera with me in the skidder from now on."

The second article in Janelle's collection was from the *Bangor Daily News*. Due to diligent assistance from Elizabeth Stevens (special collections, Bangor Public Library), the date, full title and page number were found, although they were missing from Janelle's copy.[46] Reporter Pat Shaw filed this with the headline "Viewers Report 'Sasquatch' Seen." James Ross, then a game warden, was dispatched to the scene by Warden Supervisor Larry Cummings, who believed the creature was nothing but an angry female bear defending its cub. (A theory attributed to Ross in the later *Somerset Reporter*

---

[*] Remember that Janelle mentioned that the description was altered from her father's original quote so is likely to be at least partially inaccurate. For instance, he did not describe the fur as being "yellowish."

article.) The reporter mentions that Ross "feels that the man in question 'definitely saw something,'" but Ross says, "It is very possible that someone put [the tracks] there as a joke."

The number of sightings is played down in the *Bangor Daily News* article, totaling "at least two," both from the same witness—although later in the article readers are given a conflicting account: "Ross confirmed that *several complaints* have been reported, all within the same general area." (Emphasis mine.) When I spoke to Ross in March 2019, he said, "I do remember having other people telling me that they'd seen something. But there was no evidence at all to back it up," whereas in the Moody case, physical traces were found at the site. The *Bangor Daily News* article described the footprints differently, quoting Ross as saying they were "approximately 14 to 15 inches in length, six inches wide, and having four toes." The *Somerset Reporter* article reports them as "roughly 18 inches long."

Both articles feature quotes from game wardens exhorting people to stop going into the area with guns in search of the creature, with Ross warning, "This has got to stop; someone is going to get hurt."

As I untangled the maze of misinformation in the articles, Janelle clarified the color information for me: "I remember dad saying that first day that it was dark colored with [long] gray, red and light brown streaks, which is what I saw. Dad said the face was dark colored and rather flat, and the top of the head wasn't as rounded as our heads are, it was more pointed—not drastically but more than ours. I remember my uncle saying the same thing."

Janelle's dad thought the creatures had been driven out of the deep woods by large fires in May and June 1977. This theory meshes with a mysterious hint I found in a Gene Letourneau article—a tantalizing thorn in my side since finding it years before. I had been looking for Janelle's account from two different directions without realizing her family's sightings were at the center of it all.

The fires Janelle mentioned were disastrous for large parts of the state. As of a May 30 article in the *Kennebec Journal*, "Workers were still dousing a 2,000 acre forest fire at Lake Moxie in Somerset County, but officials were confident that the three-day-old blaze was under control."[47] A month or so later, famed Maine outdoors writer Gene Letourneau opened his article, "Was It a Bear or Bigfoot?"[48] with this to say:

> *Was an unusually large animal akin to Bigfoot driven out of its lair by the Lake Moxie forest fire? That question is being circulated from Canaan to*

Jackman these days with reports that an awesome animal has been sighted since the fire.

None of the sightings has been officially confirmed. But some have come from reliable sources, like a farmer in Canaan who described the animal as "bear-like" but taller than any he's ever seen and covered with a strange texture of hair rather than fur.

The Lake Moxie fire burned about 2,000 acres within which are a number of dens that most likely have been used by black bears for many years. These are in ledges found east of the Kennebec River where in past years bounty hunters used to find as many as four bears in a single den.

Can you see why I was doubly excited to hear Janelle's story? As she said to me when I visited Skowhegan in June 2019, "Kind of gives you goosebumps sometimes, when you figure the connections all out, you know?" I *do* know.

I researched the scope and timing of the Moxie Pond* fire and the Baxter State Park fire that summer, but details are elusive. I had to depend on varying information from newspaper articles of the time. In a July 2019 email, forest ranger specialist Kent Nelson gave me the disappointing news that "unfortunately, we have very little records about the 1977 fire in Baxter State Park," in part because annual commissioner's reports were not printed after 1976. However, he and Cheri Bellavance, both of the Maine Forest Service, were able to provide me with satellite images delineating the general outline of the two conflagrations. This allowed me to locate them on a map.

The timing of the Moxie Pond fire fit the onset of events in the Skowhegan area. The distance of the fire site from the Skowhegan activity was about thirty miles as the crow flies, not an unusual distance for a large mammal to travel, given typical black bear ranges. Even a healthy human can walk twenty to thirty miles in a day.[49] To speculate—why wouldn't creatures fleeing the fire head for the westward oasis of Flagstaff Lake and Bigelow Preserve? It could simply be that the sprawling ridges of Maine mountains, which start at about that point, were a visible deterrent, and animals would avoid these potentially extreme obstacles. The boggy lowlands could present a more appealing sanctuary.

In terms of barriers to foot travel, Moxie Pond swings down and eastward from the location of the fire, making a natural funnel south from the fire site. The Kennebec River, flowing southward, a bit to the west, spreads into the elongated body of Wyman Lake, which would effectively route escapees even more tightly southward from the west, reinforced by the

---

* Referred to by Letourneau as Lake Moxie rather than its official name of Moxie Pond.

parallel manmade deterrent of Maine State Route 201. If something fled south from the fire site, avoiding the north-south line of natural barriers on either side, following the wetlands and waterways, which stretch south from Moxie Pond, and areas of lower elevation away from the mountains to the west, it could find itself in the Skowhegan area, a very pleasant place to land indeed.

But what of the current state of affairs? In the summer of 2019, to my fascination, one man's Facebook post about a chance sighting enticed a number of other people to come forward with reports of their own, their neighbors' and family members'. On June 4, 2019, a post appeared on a Skowhegan community board about a brief but staggering encounter. Out on a service call on a dirt road, the eyewitness missed the address on his work order. He reached a dead end with water and mud in front of him and no option but to back up in a nearby drive. There he saw "what looked like a large man covered in hair walking across the yard at the back of the camp, and down over a bank out of sight." An uncle in nearby Canaan told him of other sightings dating to the 1970s, including those of Janelle's family.

The man contacted Janelle and with her help posted his encounter on Facebook, in the hopes that he could find out what others in the area knew. By mid-July 2019, the post had garnered 295 comments (not including the comments deleted for being rude). Many comments added information, including at least a dozen other sightings and encounters from the immediate area. Janelle was amazed—for years she had been trying to get folks to open up, and it had been like pulling teeth, but something about the timing of his post was right, and the floodgates released.

From the information in the posted comments and some follow-up messaging with people involved, Janelle collected multiple sighting locations. With a sense of vindication after years of waiting and with growing excitement, she mapped out a giant loop winding through the area. A week and a half later (through the kindness of my friend Salli, ever willing for wild rides in the name of *Strange Maine* investigations), I was able to meet Janelle in person. We spent over two hours driving around in her truck to see for ourselves how connected all these locations are and how they tie in with her family's encounters. Here was a real connect-the-dots. As I sat in the passenger seat, pages from DeLorme's *Maine Atlas and Gazetteer* on my lap, tracing our progress and noting points of interest, I watched the loop form, expanding north and east from the center of Skowhegan.

But that wasn't the wildest thing of all. As we pulled up the drive of the camp where the sighting had occurred days before, Janelle casually revealed that this was the exact camp where her son and his friends had their encounter in 2002. It was with an added thrill that I looked down the drop-off and across that sprawling bog, hazy with spring rain and waiting mosquitoes.

It does seem that what started in the 1970s in the Skowhegan area continues today.

9

LYNNE COLLETT

Something Watching in the Woods

LITTLE RIVER ROAD, BERWICK
YORK COUNTY, AUGUST 1977

In 1977, Lynne was a teenager in Berwick, alongside the Maine–New Hampshire border at the very southernmost tip of the state. Years later, this incident is clear in her mind. This is a Class A sighting, the first report to come to me from York County.

IT WAS A HOT evening in early August 1977. Lynne was babysitting, keeping an eye on four youngsters. The kids, ranging from six to ten years old, were playing a rowdy game of hide-and-seek in the woods beside the house. Two lived here, where she was staying as a friend of the family. She had helped watch them ever since moving in earlier that summer. The other two were visiting while their parents were inside socializing.

The sun sank and shadows grew. The game was quiet as the kids hid from whoever was "it." Lynne was surprised when one of the boys came up and told her, "Something big is behind the house."

Lynne asked him, "Like a moose?"

The boy replied, "No, moose don't stand on two legs."

Like any good babysitter, Lynne squashed the flash of panic inside her and said instead, "Wow, well do you think you could show me?" With a wide-eyed nod, the boy took her hand and led her to the corner of the house.

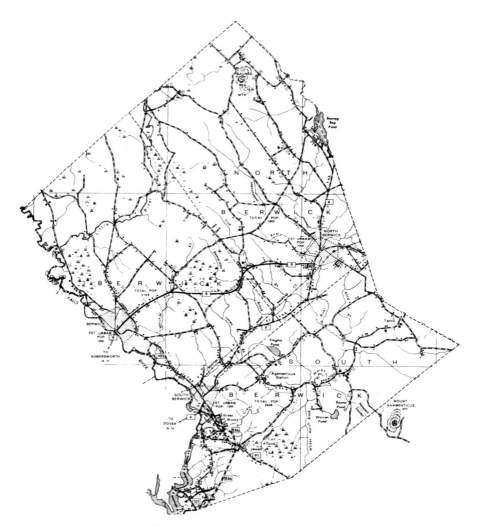

A map of the Berwick area. Maine General Highway Atlas, *1959*.

Lo and behold, there was indeed a huge creature visible just inside the woods. It was watching the kids laugh and shriek as the usual uproar of the "finding" stage of hide-and-seek erupted. Lynne could see enough to know it was not human. It was huge, covered in long dark hair with longer-than-human arms. It held onto a tree and swayed back and forth in a slow, preoccupied motion as it watched the kids play. She thought it was curious about all the noise. Lynne was curious too, but more than that, she was *terrified*.

The boy looked up at Lynne, and she put her finger to her lips. She whispered to him, "Go get the rest of the kids and tell them I said it's time to go in." He nodded and ran off. She realized she hadn't told him not to mention the creature, and her heart leaped. She didn't want the kids to panic. She wanted to get them inside safely. As the boy ran toward his friends, the creature heard the movement and turned to look directly at Lynne. In her head the words rang out silently, "Holy mother of God, I know what you are." She stood frozen, watching it. To her relief, the kids all headed back to the house as if nothing was happening. As they finished thundering up the stairs behind her, she thawed her petrified limbs enough to move and carefully, slowly stepped back and ran inside too.

The parents looked up from their card game, surprised everyone was in so early. Lynne explained they'd been eaten alive by mosquitoes. She sat down on the couch and turned on the television, keeping an ear on the boys playing in the nearby bedroom. She was dozing when the card game ended, and the visiting family headed home.

Lynne had little inclination to go to her bedroom in the basement. The basement door had been open all day. What if that thing had gotten in? It hadn't looked vicious, but remembering its size and appearance filled her with trepidation. She lingered in front of the television rather than chance an encounter in the dark downstairs. Suddenly, something outside gave an unbelievable howl, and she jumped off the couch. She ran to the parents' room and knocked on the door. Asleep, they didn't answer, so she ran to the bathroom window to look outside. Everything was dark and silent.

She stayed on the couch all night, eventually falling asleep. The next morning, she peered outside and then went into the yard to look around. The only thing out of place was an empty cheese doodle bag torn apart, but that could have been any animal. She didn't see any tracks in the grass.

Within a week, she moved out of the house to stay with other friends.

Lynne didn't tell anyone about this encounter until years later, when she and a friend began watching episodes of *Finding Bigfoot*. She tried contacting the young boy, now a grown adult, as his sister was a longtime friend of hers. He didn't want to talk about it.

Lynne and I started emailing back and forth in January 2018. What had she noticed in those frozen moments after it turned around to look at her? She told me its expression wasn't threatening, just curious. Its face had hair on it but wasn't heavily or completely covered. The facial skin was dark brown. She does not remember seeing ears and recalls the nose was "squished like a

Hide-and-seek with unplanned guests. *Illustration by Michelle Y. Souliere.*

gorilla's." The eyes were big. She didn't remember seeing the whites of the eyes, just the impression that the eyes were large.

Its body was covered with hair, some matted, "a deep rust and dark brown," varying between three to eight inches in length. She saw it from the side, and when it turned toward her, she saw some of its front. Its hand, hanging down at its side, was large with long fingers. There were no clues about gender. It looked about seven feet tall. "I would compare [its shape] to a body builder's. Large broad chest and slimmer from the waist down." This broadness of form continued from the chest and shoulders up through the neck area, where she remembers the hair being longest. Lynne remembers thinking to herself, "Wow, he has no neck—how is he turning his head?"

Its posture was upright but with knees somewhat bent. It was pursing its lips as it watched, "like when you throw a kiss," puckering its lips in and out quickly as it watched the children's antics in puzzlement. I asked her if she noticed any odor. She recalled earlier in the evening the kids commented on a strong unpleasant odor, and they all laughed together when Lynne teased them that whoever got caught first in the game had to find the mess and clean it up, whatever it was.

She remembered a prior incident that gained significance in retrospect. She and the boys went to feed some geese at a neighbor's house. The two boys rode bikes with Lynne on foot. Heading home, they asked if they could cut through the woods. As home was so close, there seemed nothing wrong with this. Lynne agreed, if they promised not to stop and play along the way, as their father was due home any minute.

Forty-five minutes later, the boys had yet to arrive. When their dad arrived home, he asked Lynne where they were. When Lynne explained, he panicked, and said, "No! They are not supposed to go through the woods! They know better!" He took off to find them, eventually emerging with them safe. Taking Lynne aside, he told her the woods were off-limits to the boys. "There are animals in those woods that can hurt them. They are not allowed in them ever again." Very seriously, he added, "And neither are you, do you understand me?"

Lynne agreed and apologized. Everything went back to normal. The incident wasn't brought up again, but Lynne never forgot about it. Seeing him so visibly shaken was enough to set that rule in stone for her, forevermore. At the time, she assumed he was talking about bears. A few weeks later, after her own encounter, she thought perhaps he had been hinting at something else entirely.

10

JOHN HAWKINS

In the Path of Something Big

MAINE–NEW HAMPSHIRE BORDER NEAR FRYEBURG, WHITE MOUNTAINS,
OXFORD COUNTY
CIRCA 1978

Several episodes relayed to me are not clear-cut Class A sightings but contain details compelling enough to make you scratch your head, or if you were the one in the tent, enough to make you remember the incident and the terror you felt for the rest of your life. This is one of these Class B sightings.

IT WAS LATE SUMMER, and John Hawkins was done with work for the week. It was time to pick up a lady friend and leave hot and hectic jobs behind, escaping through Oxford County to the cool, quiet White Mountains for a camping trip. It was high season, and all he wanted to do was get away from the crowds that ironically came to Maine to escape themselves—the disruptive but economically important cycle of seasonal tourism in Maine. He and his date left late, driving west as daylight retreated. Darkness falls quickly in the mountains. It was time to stop while they could still see to pitch their tent. They didn't need much, just a place to lay their heads.

They pulled off onto a gravel road less than one hundred yards long, maybe a plow turnoff, common in those mountain roads. They headed up a steep game trail, stopping at a tiny level clearing. The tent left just enough room for them to walk around and get the pegs in. They settled into their sleeping bags. The last of the long summer day's light faded around them. It was sometime after 8:00 p.m.

Lying on your back in a tent surrounded by trees is singularly relaxing. Breezes move through the woods, and birds call out their last songs. Small pinecones drop into the underbrush off to the side as a squirrel scampers along, headed for its treetop perch. Night slowly slips down and tucks you in as the twilight glow ebbs.

Something, however, was making a surprising amount of noise on the hill above. They looked at each other: "What is that?" Both shook their heads, puzzled. It was so heavy that they could feel the impact of each footfall vibrating the ground beneath their sleeping bags. John almost thought it was a bear, except a bear runs on four padded feet. It sounded much more aggressive than a black bear. *Pound, pound, pound.* John pulled out his pistol and gave his hunting knife to his companion, telling her, "Whatever it is, we go out fighting."

It came down the trail, passed their tent and gave a grunt of surprise. It almost sounded like a person with a low bull alligator growl to its voice as it said, "Uh!" They listened, scared to death. The sound had come from high in the air. Whatever it was, it was tall. They heard it reverse toward their tent and stop. What was it doing just standing there? Then it walked around their tent in the narrow margin between the thin nylon walls and the underbrush. It stepped slowly, one foot after the other. The nylon above their heads pushed in where its hand rubbed around on it. The thing was huge.

John and his friend silently panicked. It circled their tent four times, with its hand on the fabric high above them. Finally, it paused, and as they held their breath, it went downhill, resuming its interrupted journey.

They remained in the dark tent, shaken. John's companion wanted to run to the car. John tried to reason with her: "No. We can't see this thing. We don't know what it is. It could easily attack us on the way down. Let's stay in the tent. Worst comes to worst, I can back it off with a few bullets. If we go down there, it could be waiting for us." It took them a long time to get any sleep.

They had planned to spend the whole weekend in the White Mountains. "We just got in the car and got the hell out of there. We rode all the way back to southern Maine, and I don't think we even talked," John recalled when I interviewed him via telephone in 2015. "We were both just shattered. We were so afraid. I don't think we talked ever again. I think that was our one and only date."

"It was just…out of our world. We just did not know what could've done that.…Because it just didn't *fit* anything."

John has faced many intimidating animals in his life. Down south in the swamps where he grew up working with cattle, extra vigilance toward predators was essential, especially during calving times. He hunted deer and wild boar. He even encountered a panther, but it's been a long time since he's wanted to hunt. "When I grew up down south, hunting was part of the culture, but as I grew older, I appreciated more about the animal world."

He doesn't remember any particular smell from that night. He certainly didn't stick around to look for tracks. He is unsure of precisely where the encounter occurred, but it was right on the Maine–New Hampshire border between Fryeburg and Conway, his usual camping route. He estimates they hiked about forty yards up the game trail from the end of the short gravel road. He is hopeful that the area avoided development. The local deer population would be a good food source. He laments it would have been a lot easier to go looking in 1978, if only he had thought of it then—maybe during the daytime, maybe with a few friends.

Looking back, he is tempted to draw conclusions. "That thing—it was obvious the way that thing came down that trail in the twilight that this was its territory. It didn't miss a step. It came down there very fast." The creature was breaking branches as it moved around on the slope, stepping on them as it walked, unconcerned about being heard. It had waited until it started getting dark, so it probably had good night vision. He doesn't think it was a known Maine mammal. "It did not fit bear, moose, deer, anything.…A moose just couldn't do it, the rack would've been all up in the branches. And there was absolutely no way around that tent that a moose could have circled. Just barely enough room to put a three-person tent down, and that was about it." And the hand pushing in and moving around on the tent fabric continues to astonish him. "You could see it was a hand. It was huge."

It wasn't until 2015 that he began to turn the incident over in his memory. Some online research provided him with other reports, including Peter Samuelson's sighting about thirty miles southwest of John's encounter, near Connor Pond in New Hampshire.[50] This gave John some validation. Back then, he associated these creatures with exotic places like Nepal, like the Yeti he read about in a *Reader's Digest* article.[51] He didn't think Bigfoot could be local, but things are different now, with *Finding Bigfoot* and others investigating every corner for mystery primates. Today, he's sure he encountered Bigfoot that night. "It could not have been anything else."

11

JOHN DOE (AROOSTOOK COUNTY)

Nighttime Visitor

E Plantation (Township E), Aroostook County
Circa 1983

This is another Class B sighting with interesting similarities to John Hawkins's case. Again, this case lacks a straightforward visual but imagine being the one lying awake in that tent. These events still haunt John today. Additional incidents involve family members, so while I retain his information in my files, readers must be content with his anonymity.

It was a summer night in 1983 or 1984. John was around eleven years old and was sleeping over at his cousin's. Their campsite wasn't remote—only seventy-five feet from his cousin's house in their large backyard. The landscape was familiar and homey. Nearby was a pasture and a barn where the family kept their horse, plus a second pasture and larger field across the road. They camped in a big yellow tent with an exterior metal frame. It was set up underneath a tree, overhung by an old bug zapper, providing a continual hum and a reassuring nightlight. The tent seemed huge to the two boys— tall enough that an adult could stand up in the middle. On each side of its peak, the tent angled out like a roof before dropping to the ground in a house-like shape.

The cousins fell asleep late, as usual. Deep in the night, John woke up to hear a thumping sound. *Bump, bump, bump…*pause…*bump, bump, bump…*

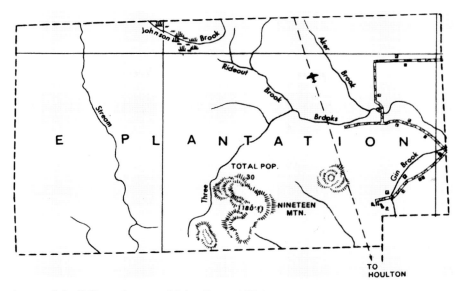

A map of the E Plantation area. Maine General Highway Atlas, *1959.*

pause, over and over again. It wasn't loud, just enough to wake him up. It was audible above their radio's volume, playing low between the cricket chirps and other Aroostook nighttime noises. The noise went on through a few songs but eventually stopped, and he fell back asleep.

Later John woke up again to a different sound, like rocks being hit together. He thought it was the horse, restless in its nearby barn stall. The night resumed its usual quiet, and he went to sleep again. The next day, he discovered that the horse hadn't been in the barn. It was in the pasture across the road. It was puzzling, but he set those thoughts aside as the day went on.

Later that summer, he and his cousin walked down a wooded dirt road near the house. They could hear something keeping pace alongside them in the woods. The road emerged into a clearing. Whatever it was, it couldn't follow farther without showing itself, which seemed to infuriate it. It gave a growling sound. They ran for home. Even if it was just a coyote, they weren't going to stick around—not this close to dark.

They had many sleepovers in the tent that summer. One night after the spooky growl incident, they lugged their gear out to the tent again and stayed up late talking as usual. They heard John's aunt arrive home from working at the McCain's potato factory and knew it must be about 11:30 p.m., the cue to finally sack out.

A little later, John woke up. Over his cousin's snoring, he heard something moving outside the tent. He lay still. A rapid sniffing sound, as if a dog was outside, came next. He thought, "Maybe it's a coyote." He held himself perfectly still, listening between the radio's low mumbling and his cousin's snores. He couldn't hear anything that sounded like footsteps, just that sniffing noise.

Something brushed up against the tent. In the dim glow from the bug zapper, he saw the tent fabric move as something pushed lightly on its side. Now he was scared. He desperately wished his cousin would stop snoring so he wouldn't give their presence away to the thing outside.

Overhead, a shadow reached its long arm halfway across the tent's top. What looked like a big hand grazed the fabric of the tent as the shadow moved past and then away. It had put its fingers to the tent tentatively, as if it expected it to be hot to the touch. Silence returned. John lay still for what felt like hours, heart pounding, too afraid to move or wake his snoring cousin. Eventually, the late hour got the better of him, and he fell back asleep.

Being a kid, it was relatively easy to forget these events in good company, wild in the Maine summer. He wasn't scared to go into the woods. He grew up fishing and hunting without anything ever happening again.

It wasn't until he was almost thirty that it returned to haunt him. Stressed out and working long hours, he was plagued by nightmares about the encounter. The nightmares included familiar childhood settings. He would find himself in the fields his family traveled through to cut winter woodstove fuel. In the dream, he knew something unseen was there. He could hear it in the woods alongside the fields. Then the thing would scream, still hidden in the trees, and he would wake up.

These dreams went on until he met his wife. As he told her everything, old questions arose. What had visited their backyard campsite? She encouraged him to research similar encounters in the area, and as he wrote to me, "the rest is history." Since then, he has run across some accounts but thinks most people in Aroostook aren't open to talking about the subject.

When he asked his siblings, some had similar experiences that they had never talked about. One occurred when he was too small to remember it himself. The family was living in a mobile home near where John later had his own encounter. He was still small enough to share the top bunk with his older sister. One night, she woke up and saw what she described as a monkey or an ape looking in the window at them.

Around the same time, his six- or seven-year-old brother noticed a big rock nearby—a rock that stood up on two legs and walked into the woods. Later,

Curious about sleeping children. *Illustration by Michelle Y. Souliere.*

they were outside playing when his mom and his aunt started yelling to come inside. His mother held a shotgun. Later, she told him she'd seen something black visible in the brush around the yard. She thought it was a bear but wasn't sure. John mentioned it was unusual for a black bear to approach a group of six kids playing loudly outside in the summer heat. As an adult, he asked his mother again what it was—could it have been a Sasquatch? She told him it could've been, as she never really knew what it was.

These incidents occurred interwoven with everyday life. The family involved had multiple brushes with an unidentifiable creature. Collectively, as adults they still question what it was that they saw and heard as children growing up in an Unorganized Territory of northern Maine.

12

JOHN DOE (PENOBSCOT COUNTY)

A Brief Startling Encounter

HUDSON, PENOBSCOT COUNTY
CIRCA 1985

Like others who encountered the unexpected during their childhood, John Doe cannot forget. His early years were spent in rural Hudson, a small town north of Bangor directly west of a swath of wilderness, including the mammoth sprawl of Alton Bog. John was referred to me by author and friend Nomar Slevik. This is a Class A sighting from Penobscot County.

JOHN WAS ABOUT EIGHT years old when he was playing in his grandmother's backyard next door. It wasn't a workday, and all the adults were gathered in her kitchen. It was overcast, a gloomy, mid-season day—not too hot, not too cold but a little dull and drab. He was monkeying around on his grandmother's timber-frame clothesline, using it as a jungle gym. He was hanging from his arms on the clothesline when he looked up to see something very tall and covered in black fur walking on two legs across the clearing at the back of the yard.

He hung there, astonished. The creature turned its head and looked at him and then continued on its way as John jumped down, hitting the ground, running pell-mell for the house. He told everyone inside, "There's a big thing that just walked across the backyard, and it was completely solid black, and it was taller than Jimmy." The adults piled out to take a look, but there was nothing left to see, and that was that.

A map of the Hudson area. Maine General Highway Atlas, *1959.*

   Their friend Jimmy was the tallest person any of them knew, six and a half feet tall. John wanted the adults to understand that the creature was noticeably bigger—"professional basketball player height and size, maybe a little thicker," around seven feet tall, and "the arms were noticeably long." It walked upright on two legs, long arms swinging naturally, with a little bit of forward lean in its momentum. "I remember that the hands were long. Definitely not paws. It was a very long hand."

   "It was very humanoid, very human-shaped," he recalls, but "it didn't seem to have much of a neck," making the shoulders look high by comparison. The area between its shoulders and the sides of its head was shrouded by longer hair. The overcast gloom of the day let him see little detail in that fleeting moment. He likened it to "looking at something wrapped in

An unexpected interruption. *Illustration by Michelle Y. Souliere.*

construction paper. You know how black construction paper is kind of dull, almost like it absorbs light." The creature crossed the yard about fifty to sixty feet away, headed from behind his parents' property across his grandparents' yard, continuing east.

Beyond the initial alarm, he didn't tell anyone else for many years, "because to me it didn't look like the Patterson-Gimlin image. And when I was a kid, that's the only image I had to go with." The coloration was different, the physiognomy was less bull-headed and top-heavy than the Patterson-Gimlin example. But in recent years, he realized many others had sightings that didn't match that well-known ideal either, "so I felt more comfortable in saying, 'Yeah, I guess I did see a Bigfoot'" after all.

He grew up surrounded by rural pursuits. "I was constantly in trees, on roofs, in the hayloft of my barn—just everywhere. I ran everywhere, belly-crawled under everything and was never afraid to get dirty or climb higher." The trails his family walked and foraged were a mix of game trails, power lines and old logging roads. There were chicken coops in the yard and trails that stretched for acres into the woods behind, where every year, huge patches of blackberries yielded their sweet harvest. "We had loads of apple trees, blackberry bushes, raspberry bushes," and there were plenty of gardens and crops in the neighborhood.

The area is still rural, although since his family moved away, more homes have been built. The town's population has almost doubled since 1980, when it totaled 797.[52] Hudson is peppered with little streams. Pushaw Lake stretches for seven and a half miles alongside the town to its east. A quick glimpse at satellite imagery shows a liberal smattering of swamps in the area too. As he lightly mentions, "It's a pretty soggy town."

I asked him if the encounter affected his attitude toward the outdoors, but he thinks the adults' immediate response minimized any long-term effect. When they didn't see anything themselves, their due diligence was done, and they no longer treated it seriously. Since the adults weren't worried or scared, it didn't occur to him to remain frightened, and life went on as usual. "I did read loads of monster books after that. My grandmother and I always had a great connection and loved talking about weird stuff."

The event remained dormant in the back of his mind, only putting its cold nose on his spine when odd things happened. "I remember hearing loud voices that sounded like arguing a couple of times, and it was just explained away as people in the woods hunting illegally....Occasionally a lone person would happen to walk out into our horse pasture and turn around and go back into the woods." He added, "I don't recall being scared often but certainly had times that I felt I was being watched."

Around the end of 2017, he spoke with his great-aunt about his memories of this incident, and she told him that her father (in the late 1890s, he estimates) "used to fish the Kenduskeag Stream often. He would walk from Bangor to the town of Kenduskeag, fishing the whole way. "Her father told her how the "black people who live in the woods" would watch him sometimes, in a way that sounded spooky and familiar to John. He was unable to get her to say any more on the topic, though it was pretty clear that in saying *black* she wasn't referring to people of color.

In recent years, his curiosity has given him the perfect excuse to get outside and camp as much as he can. If the worst a Bigfoot sighting can do is encourage you to go camping more, I'd say that's pretty awesome.

13

THE DUNPHYS

Across the River and into the Woods

I had tried to get the word out that I wanted to record people's Maine Bigfoot encounters with little response, so in early 2016, I wrote a press release. Articles appeared in the *Lewiston Daily Sun*[53] and in the *Bangor Daily News*,[54] thanks to the kind interest of some excellent local reporters. Mike Dunphy Sr. contacted me after reading one of these. I interviewed him via phone in January 2016 and a few days later talked to his son, Mike Dunphy Jr., as well.

This is a Class A sighting and my first Aroostook County report. Not only was there a clear visual validation of the subject of the encounter on a sunny day with no obstructions, but there were also two witnesses.

It was a gorgeous day in late May—Memorial Day weekend, in fact. May in Maine has a particular quality of light and air. The blue sky, the sun, the high white clouds here and there—there is nothing so perfect, especially after long winter months. Mike Dunphy Sr. was having a great day. He had time off, plus his son, Mike Dunphy Jr., was on break. They both hightailed it to Island Falls, where Mike Sr. had grown up and his parents still lived. The weather was terrific, and they spent the morning visiting their favorite fishing spots. It felt almost summerlike to Mike Jr. They were far away from everything with no requirements but to enjoy themselves and maybe catch a few fish.

Noon found them on the West Branch of the Mattawamkeag River between Dyer Brook and Island Falls. Just upstream was a shallow section of the river, where an old tote road cut across to logging sections and camps deeper in the woods. They waded into the river slowly, figuring out the good spots before casting. Like most good outdoorsmen, both were in the habit of scanning the nearby landscape. There was movement across the river.

Something walked out of the woods into the open, crossing the old tote road, walking upright, on two legs. It was tall and completely covered in dark brown hair. Mike Sr. noticed it had long arms. Its posture wasn't quite the same as a human's. Something about it was a little different, Mike Jr. thought. It turned and noticed them too. It paused. The two men looked at it, and it looked at them. Then it walked off into the woods, north to wherever it was headed.

The Dunphys looked at each other. They reeled up their lines, turned, walked out of the river to where they had parked their truck and drove back to the family homestead in town. They didn't talk. They didn't mention what they'd seen to the elder Dunphys when they arrived home safely. It wasn't until years later while watching television that they turned and looked at each other—their experience tallied with what was on the screen.

Now, twenty-plus years later, they are more comfortable talking about what happened that spring day. It still surprises them—you can hear it in their voices as they remember the event. Mike Jr. admits, "It definitely freaked us out. I wasn't scared, but there was something curious and curiously bizarre about it." At the time, he never felt unsafe or threatened—the occurrence was just weird. His father remembers the jolt of astonishment when they made eye contact as the scariest part of it—both parties frozen, staring at each other across the river. "It didn't call out or make any noise. It was as startled as much by us being there as we were by it. It was trying to keep a low profile, I'd say—go undetected. Didn't show any aggression. It was surprised to see us." Mike Jr. agrees. "I think if we weren't looking over there, if our eyes didn't glance over there, we never would have seen it." He notes that noise from the fast-flowing springtime river covered any sound of the creature's approach.

Mike Sr. wishes he had crossed over to go look for footprints at the time, but "it startled us so much that my son and myself looked at one another and never said a word to one another as to, 'Did you see what I just saw?' Because we both saw it at the same time. We just looked at one another, turned, walked out of the river, walked back to the truck, and drove back to town....We were just in shock." Mike Sr. estimates that the creature was about 250 feet across the tote road from where they stood on the other side of the river. The clear-cut of the old tote road adjoins a grassy delta area that splits the river from the eddy or meander, and that's where the unexpected visitor had come out of the woods.

Both agree it was not a bear. It was tall, "taller than any man." Mike Sr. remembers it being around eight feet. Mike Jr. estimates more conservatively that it was well over six feet but not exceeding seven feet, with an impressive build. "It wasn't slender. It wasn't obese. It was full-bodied, almost Rob Gronkowski-ish. Very thick and strong." It moved with a methodical, smooth rhythm, and Mike Jr. recalls that while upright, the way it moved was different somehow. "The posture wasn't what you would expect from a human being."

It had a completely hairy body. Mike Jr. described it as being "on the darker side of brown," longer than a bear's coat and "shaggy," not all the same length. This was another element that cleared the board for misidentification for Mike Jr. "It was all fur and hair, it wasn't 'Okay, there's a guy, maybe he's got a hat on or something.'" The creature was not a human being. It's clear he feels frustrated he didn't observe more at the time, but he won't speculate. Mike Sr. remembers, "It had a face; it didn't have a snout," one more reason it wasn't a bear. "It definitely didn't have a prominent nose," Mike Jr. says, echoing his father's observation. "I remembered the face seemed to be mostly covered in hair. I believe that there was some eye contact there, however briefly. Now, I couldn't tell you any of the details of the eyes from that distance. But there was some level of contact there. He knew we were there."

Mike Sr. has fished that spot many times since, as has his son. Each time, he looks across the river again, hoping for a repeat performance, but his reclusive neighbor hasn't obliged. He's taken friends there and told them about it. He stays at his hunting camp in the woods, which is even more remote, spending time out in the woods at night. "I'm not frightened of the woods, nor do I ever think of him being there, back in that section, where I am."

Mike Jr. feels similarly but adds, "I still haven't crossed to go over there. I think [my father has] crossed and explored there....He's got it all figured out, I guess." Mike Jr. considers it to have been an interesting experience. "I still look back on it as something that was very cool. Could I prove that it was [Bigfoot]? No, I couldn't do that. [At the time] I certainly wasn't going to cross and go look for a track or anything like that." He knows what he saw. "I fall back on all the time prior to it and since then that I've spent in the woods, the things that I've seen. I've been charged by a moose before; I've been close enough to these things to know that maybe I shouldn't be [that close to them]....Of course it was the era before smartphones or anything else. There's no photo proof, right?"

Two men and a Bigfoot met in the woods and went their own ways. Now you know about it too.

14

HANNAH HOLBROOK

Out of the Sudden Silence

CAMDEN HILLS STATE PARK, WALDO COUNTY
LATE SUMMER CIRCA 1996

This is another encounter that, though lacking visual validation, ticks a few boxes for interesting details. Twenty years after the fact, when Hannah* emailed me, it still bothered her. In the greater scheme of things, this narrative might be peripheral (in fact, the witness started her first email to me, "Not sure if this is helpful"), but I include it because of proximity, both chronological and geographical, to the Northport episode that follows. This is a Class B sighting from Waldo County.

HANNAH AND HER DOG, Annie, arrived at the Lincolnville trailhead, ready to take advantage of the shady woods on a summer day. She preferred these quiet trails over the crowded Camden trailheads. It was high summer, and the woods were alive with birdcalls. A pileated woodpecker hammered away, adding its staccato beat to the happy ruckus. The scent of dry leaves and soil, hot in the late August sun, saturated the still air. She was excited to explore some old stone walls she'd noticed previously.

Hannah and her dog reached the turnoff to the Sky Blue Trail, about two miles into the woods. There was an immediate hush. She felt uneasy as the dead silence flattened the landscape of normal bird sounds. She debated continuing to the stone wall visible ahead or turning back. She slowed her

---

* The eyewitness has chosen to use a pseudonym for the sake of privacy.

Part of the rocky trails in Camden Hills State Park. *Photo by Michelle Y. Souliere.*

pace and listened carefully. Her dog, Annie, usually far ahead, hovered behind Hannah as they inched up the familiar path.

Hannah was shocked by a rotten egg smell of sulfur and thought, "Wow, I haven't smelled that since chemistry class." The loud nearby sound of wood hitting wood startled her in the silence. The echoing hits were distinct, not a woodpecker's *ratatat-tat*. She looked around. Was it a deer knocking its antlers? The sound didn't match anything familiar at all.

Annie pressed herself to the ground, cowering. The rotten egg smell engulfed Hannah. She turned on her heels and retreated, almost running when she reached the access road. Thinking back on it later, she said, "If something was moving behind us and following us down the road, I had no idea; I never looked back. I was praying I would see another person [ahead on the trail], and I think I was gibbering."

She has thought over these events many times since. While she admits Annie is a "cream puff" of a dog and could've been responding to Hannah's own unease, it still doesn't explain what happened. "Before we turned back, I could see the whites of her eyes, and she was shaking. She continued to shake long after we got into the car." Hannah herself was shaking so badly that she dropped the car keys in the dirt at the car door, like something out of a horror movie. "I think by then my teeth were chattering," she added. What lingers for her, even today, is her "absolute sense of fear and the need to take flight." Not what one expects from a perfect summer day.

As she told me in a 2016 email, "I've gone back and forth with myself for years over this, and I've just come to the conclusion that it was a weird encounter, that for a very few moments I had enormously heightened senses, that my dog may or may not have experienced the same thing and that the fight or flight survival instinct is alive and well within me." In the mid-1990s, while aware of the concept of Sasquatch, she didn't know anything about behaviors associated with sightings, such as wood-knocks and odors. All she knew was the bewildering and immediate reaction of abject fear at that moment. It was as instantaneous "as if you were at your computer and looked up and there was a man with an axe standing behind you." Just BAM! "GO!"

Many years later, while reading an account written by Loren Coleman, she realized her experience might have a context outside of a simple freak-out. Even now, she is reluctant to assume a Sasquatch was present so close to the hum of civilization. But she reported it, just in case it was helpful. And sitting at her keyboard typing responses to my follow-up questions was enough to make her sweat, just thinking about it.

It wasn't until two years later, when I interviewed a person who had an even weirder experience about five miles northeast of Hannah's just over a year after her encounter, that I examined the area more closely. In spite of the human population that clings to the coast in this area, the region is interlaced with substantial green spaces and wild ways that would allow reticent creatures to travel in relative safety.

15

STEPHEN LOMBARDO JR.

A Bad Accident, or Something out of the *X-Files*

Northport, Waldo County
Circa November 1997

It was February 2018. I had two interviews scheduled that night. One was with Stephen Lombardo Jr. It was a wild card—all I knew was that he had seen something in Northport back in the '90s. He was another eyewitness referred by fellow investigator Nomar Slevik. Stephen's story turned out to be the strangest I heard while writing this book, but I didn't have time to think about it yet, because the phone rang for my next interview, which turned out to be the longest one I did, so I guess it was a night for breaking personal records.

This sighting probably falls under the category of a Class B sighting, but is in many ways unclassifiable, because it is so darn strange.

It was a dark November night. Stephen was riding the shuttle bus home from the new MBNA offices in Belfast, heading south to the Camden location MBNA had recently outgrown. It wasn't a bad deal to save on gas money and let someone else drive for a change. Their experienced bus driver was Beth, originally from Pennsylvania. Stephen sat on the passenger side, not far from the driver. They approached Point Lookout, a massive recreational complex on Ducktrap Mountain. The backside of the mountain was undeveloped, adjoining a land preserve, and deer often crossed Route 1 here due to the green corridor that ended at the water's edge.

A map of the Northport/Lincolnville area. Maine General Highway Atlas, *1959.*

Beth slowed the bus. Stephen heard her say, "Huh, must be an accident." A chain of large, dark unmarked vehicles was parked bumper to bumper on the shoulder of the already narrow road. Heavy-duty lights illuminated the empty field behind them. "They must have hit a deer," Beth added. Stephen moved closer to the window, peering into the darkness.

As the bus slowed further, Beth had the first view worth anything through the long panes of the bus's glass door. "That's a foot!" she exclaimed. Stephen got up and joined her. "Look at all the hair." Before him, visible in the gap between the wheels of two of the parked vehicles, was clearly a foot.

"What is it?" he asked Beth but couldn't believe her when she replied, "That's a Bigfoot." He found himself saying jokingly, "Well, I can't rule that out, because that is a pretty big foot." His eyes traveled over the heel, the contour of the instep, the big toe. Whatever it was, he thought, it was lying belly-down in that ditch with its foot hung up on the edge of the gully. But what arrested his gaze was the hair, clearly visible where it began around the ankles. The hair was backlit and reddish-brown. Disturbing clumps of it had fallen onto the ground next to the foot, as though knocked off by impact. Beth had to start moving the bus again, and they left the strange sight behind without answers. "I can't believe it," Beth said to herself as they drove away.

"No, you've got to be kidding me. That's not a Bigfoot," Stephen argued. But it wasn't a deer, and no evening jogger was ever that furry or ran around in November without socks or shoes on a commuter stretch of U.S. Route 1.

"I'm from Pennsylvania, and I've seen stuff like this before," Beth tried to explain.

"Come on, you're pulling my leg." Stephen countered. But Beth was dead serious, and she wasn't known for joking around. They began dissecting what they had seen. Stephen occasionally erupted into disbelieving laughter, saying, "I can't believe this." There wasn't any construction work to explain away the industrial lights. There was nobody directing traffic where the vehicles caused a bottleneck on the road, and they hadn't been there when Beth drove through about a half hour before. They had been looking for a hoof, imagining a deer collision. But instead, they saw a large bare foot and part of a hair-covered leg only a bumper's length away from them, brightly lit. These details were undeniable.

When he left the bus, Stephen asked Beth to keep her eye out on the way back. The next evening, she looked at him significantly. "You've got to hear this." He sat down next to her. "On the way back, about twenty-five minutes later, everybody's gone. And they *pressure-washed the road*." The road had been scoured clean for about twenty feet in that exact area. None of it made any more sense than before. In fact, this new information somehow made it worse.

Two decades later, during our conversation, Stephen was clearly right back in that moment, sitting in the dark on the bus, seeing something unbelievable. Witnessing the aftereffects of any collision is an extremely disturbing experience, sending the mind in loops, reiterating unanswerables—what-if after what-if. He has continued to reexamine that night. About ten years ago, he tried to locate Beth, the driver. He knew roughly where she lived in Rockland, but she had apparently moved back to Pennsylvania. Riders and drivers had been on a first name basis only, and he couldn't find her in company directories, possibly because the drivers were hired independently through a CDL contractor.

At the time, there was nothing in the news about the accident. "I was hoping it wasn't a person hit, but that area of Route 1 is just a commuting area. You don't usually see people jogging or biking, especially in November at that time." Another explanation he thought of was a night-time shoot for a movie. After all, the Stephen King movie *Thinner* was filmed in Camden in 1994. But no official crew was filming in the area, according to the Maine Film Office's list.* Stephen examined his mental checklist of large Maine mammals he had seen in person: black bear, deer, moose? No, no, no. "I know what a leg looks like on a deer; it's spindly. This wasn't it. This was *big*. I've seen a bear at a close distance, up in Rangeley. I've seen that stuff."

That sudden revelation after their slow approach toward the lights and the line of vehicles had been startling. "I was looking for a hoof.…Because I was thinking it was a deer or a person that was hit. By a car, in a ditch." But that wasn't what he saw. And even though Beth came right out and said it, he could not wrap his mind around the idea of Bigfoot in Maine. Sasquatch was a West Coast creature, and "Honestly, I didn't really believe in Bigfoot."

Each time, his mind returned to the hair. He asked if I was familiar with cattails, long plants that grow in marshes all over Maine. They are topped with an unmistakable brown flower head that looks like a corndog on a stick. "You know [how] if you take and whip them, that [brown] stuff falls off in patches? It reminded me of that." At another point, he compared it to a Tweety and Sylvester cartoon, "when the gun blows up, [and] their hair blows off from their fingers." In both cases, I could see the image he was trying to convey. Cartoons and cattails are one thing, but to see that in real life must have been beyond surreal.

The other item he got stuck on was how it had been handled. The fact that the vehicles came en masse, did what they had to do and just as swiftly departed from the scene with their high-powered lighting equipment, carefully cleaning the road before they left—what did *that* mean? Their efficiency freaked him out. He traveled past on the shuttle bus, twice a day as usual, and the cleaned area was obvious. In that twenty-foot section of road, neither pavement nor its cracks showed any debris, unlike the surrounding asphalt. He visited the site and looked for indications of a collision but found nothing.

What else did he remember? He recalled the skin on the foot looked "like somebody had a suntan and dirty feet." While it was not pale, he doesn't remember the skin as being heavily pigmented or overly dark. He estimates the hair was about two and a half to three inches long. "It was shorter than a horse's mane, but it still was long enough that it was kind of fluffed out. It

---

* "Films Made in Maine," Maine Film Office, 2018, filminmaine.com. I also checked with film-making friends likely to have been aware of any guerrilla filming. Nada.

The roadside, ditch and field on US Route 1 in Northport, where Stephen Lombardo Jr. saw the mysterious nighttime convocation. *Photo by Michelle Y. Souliere.*

wasn't thick like a dog's. It was kind of wisping around if the wind hit it." He could see what looked like a couple of bald spots and thought, "This thing got hit, because it took the hair off him, whatever happened. I saw a plop of hair next to his foot. That's what caught my eye."

He didn't see anyone as they went by—just the row of tightly parked vehicles, the lights and the foot. Due to the narrowness of the road, they drove past only inches away from the parked vehicles. They couldn't see over them. He speculates there might have been people behind the vehicles, shortened by standing in the culvert. He couldn't tell what color the vehicles were, but they were dark, all the same height and parked tight. There were no identifying marks. The lamps of the lighting rig were visible over the vehicle tops, pointed down into the field beyond. They appeared to be heavy duty industrial lamps—the portable kind used at night-time construction sites.

In all the years before and since, Stephen hasn't encountered anything strange in that area. He's pretty sure this took place in 1997. He's also pretty sure it was November, as it was hunting season, and deer were on his mind. It would have been between 5:30 and 6:00 p.m., because he got off shift around 5:00. It wasn't one of the nights when he worked until 9:00, because he remembers some rush hour traffic on the road with them at various points. Maybe somebody else noticed something that night. If so, both Stephen and I would very much like to hear about it.

Point Lookout is still there. Originally built as an MBNA employee recreational center, it is now a facility for vacationers, wedding parties, conferences and retreats, boasting "387 acres of picturesque mountainside terrain overlooking Penobscot Bay."[55] The nearby field, along which the mysterious motorcade was parked, is no longer empty, sporting a newly constructed commercial venture. But who knows what lives in the woods behind?

16

MATTHEW MAXCY

Jaywalking Nightmare

Augusta Road, en route to Waldoboro, Kennebec and Lincoln Counties
January 2000

Matt Maxcy speaks from a life-long hunter's point of view. He was the first person who told me he did not want anyone thinking of his experience as a *story*. "This isn't a story. This is my encounter. This is *my* encounter. Stories are stories. This is an encounter." And he is right. People might read these accounts as stories, but they are a point in someone's life where everything changed forever.

This is a Class A sighting from the border of Kennebec and Lincoln Counties.

It was January in Maine—typically cold, covered in snow and ice, with a good three more months of the same to go. Matt Maxcy was almost to Waldoboro, driving back from Tennessee, where he'd been working. Accompanying him north was Andy, who was used to a very different climate. They were in Matt's pearly white '97 Ford Thunderbird, which just about matched the color of the snow around them and drove quiet as a snowfall. It was late morning, probably about 10:30 a.m. or so.

As in most of Maine's sparsely populated areas, the road was lined with trees. They came around a bend, a straightaway before them. Matt saw movement to the right, where the snow swept up to the tree line. At first, he just saw snow sliding from the pine branches and plopping to the ground in a soft rush. But then he saw something big and brown. Thinking this was a pretty great introduction to Maine wildlife for a guy from Tennessee, he cut his speed in half and said, "Look Andy, there's a moose." What else could something that huge be?

But it wasn't a moose. It stepped from the tree line on two legs, not four, and started down the slope. They braked to a halt as the figure strode onto the roadway a couple car lengths in front of them and stopped. Matt couldn't get Andy to talk to him, because Andy was screaming and screaming all kinds of stuff. It seemed huge as it hunkered down, trying to see past the windshield reflection. It looked like it could rip the doors off the car if it wanted to—or pick Matt up and tear him in two. The creature was the reddish-brown color of the redbone coonhounds he used to run down south when he was younger. Its coat looked kind of like bear hair, except for where it grew longer on the forearms and the lower part of the legs. It was hard to distinguish a neckline between its head and shoulders, where its long hair reminded Matt of messy rock star hair.

It bounded across the road in fewer strides than he thought possible. Matt hoped someone else would drive up and see this, but the road remained empty. When the creature reached the top of the slope on the other side, it stopped and looked at them again before vanishing into the woods, confident there was nothing the two men could do to it. It was gone. Matt could see where the creature had loped through the snow. It had happened; it was real. He felt like he was expected to suddenly believe in something as nonsensical as a leprechaun or a dragon. That thing wasn't supposed to alive—wasn't supposed to exist.

In the years since his encounter, he tells me, people have tried to say the whole thing would have been easy if it had been them: "Well, why didn't you get out and take casts of the footprints?" or "Well, *I* would've gotten out and done this and that." To them, he says, "No, no, you wouldn't have. No. Nobody would. Because you're in such shock at the mass and size of this thing. You know from the way it looks at you that if you were to even remotely upset this thing, it's going to be *game over* for you."

Matt describes it as being "too human to be considered an animal but too animal to be considered a human," like so many other eyewitnesses say. It wasn't a gorilla or an ape as we know them. He considers that it might be a woodland giant. "You could tell this thing had intelligence, and I'm not saying a gorilla doesn't have intelligence, but there was a very, very close resemblance to something like a giant man, but still not [a man]—just a little bit offset." Hair came only about halfway up its face, exposing skin that looked dark and almost bluish gray in the cold daylight. He noticed small clumps of snow dropping off its coat as it moved. The skin on its feet was the same color as its face. He could see the silhouette of its fingers and the snow caught in the fur on the back of its hands.

It looked right at him—once when it stopped in front of the car, the second time when it stopped at the top of the slope before departing into the trees. Between those two frozen moments, "it jetted across the road in huge strides, *boom, boom, boom,* and it was off….And it just gave us that look like, 'What are you gonna do?' And we didn't do anything." He laughs. "There was no way with that thing. It was a very powerful moment." Its eyes were set back under its brow and appeared black, with no whites of the eye visible. Its ears weren't apparent, perhaps because they were under shaggy hair.

Matt estimates that the creature stood about nine feet tall with a shoulder span of at least three feet. "It looked like a bodybuilder, but it didn't have the ripples in the stomach….The solar plexus was barreled out, like half-barrel solar plexus, where the stomach is." Its arms were long and massive. "It was huge. And the strength in the thing—you could tell just by looking at it that it could rip the door off my vehicle or physically pick up a man and rip him in half. It ran faster than anything I've witnessed—moose, deer, bear, elk, I've seen them all in person running. This thing ran faster than *any* of them, covered more distance faster than anything."

Matt found his life changed after the encounter. "Everybody who knows me knows that I go hunting, fishing. I would stay out in the woods by myself all night long, no guns, maybe a knife or whatever. But it's changed me. I'll get all dressed up to go hunting, and I'll go to walk out the door, and I'll look at my own wood line, and I can't do it." He understands that in general Bigfoot might be a neutral creature, but he knows if "somebody else has seen one of these just an hour earlier and shot at it or done something, and then I'm in the woods and it's angry." He can't help thinking about that risk. It's an upsetting situation to find yourself in when you've been the alpha predator all your life. "I grew up fishing, hunting, trapping, running hounds," he said. All that has changed.

Occasionally, he goes hunting with company, but he's wary now. In January 2016, a month before our interview, he and his nephew went coyote hunting near Warren. They received an unexpected response to their amplified coyote caller when they turned it off. In the silence, they heard a howling and then a roaring from a few hundred yards up the slope. It was not a coyote, and it sounded enraged. The sound was so loud that "you could feel it *through* yourself." It crescendoed over the whole valley.

From the other side came a staccato, piercing, whooping noise no coyote ever made—like something out of the deepest jungles, not the northern woods. It was more like a large gibbon's cry than anything else.* Something walked and then stopped on the slope nearby. "I want to leave, I want to leave, I want to leave!" his nephew whispered urgently. They drove down to grab the coyote caller and head home.

"It was dead quiet in there that night—dead quiet. There was no movement, nothing," he said. Matt and others had noticed the area was increasingly empty of deer. "Before, during the off-season, it would not be uncommon for us to see fifteen, maybe even twenty, thirty deer in a night in different groups walking around through the snow, leaving trails." Lately, only five or six different deer trails might appear in an evening—with no visuals whatsoever. He theorizes that the area had become a hunting territory for whatever howled that night, an idea that makes him leery of returning. "I would not attempt to shoot that thing.…Not a chance. I would not even think about shooting one of them with [my high-caliber gun, a .270], because I just don't think it would work."

Matt Maxcy takes his outdoors very seriously. Yes, he has a sense of humor and jokes around, but the outdoors is his life. "If I tell you that something like this happened, it happened. A lot of people don't want to come out with their experiences because of being ridiculed." The area where he had his first sighting is around an hour from his house. The place where he heard the vocalization is only fifteen minutes away. Both encounters were during the winter.

Matt has since collected accounts from other people. One family friend was chased by something as a teenager, back when the Old Augusta Road area was far less developed. At first, the man thought it was someone from the party he left behind. But when it came up out of the swamp at him, and he caught sight of it under the moon, he realized it wasn't human. He managed to escape and hid in a culvert, clutching a stick, his innards roiling with fear as the creature walked up and down the bank looking for him. Matt has heard all sorts of theories from folks, some of them pretty far-fetched, but when it comes down to it, he says, "What I can tell you, my personal self, is they are a flesh-and-blood creature. And they do make sounds, and they do scare the sh— out of you. Excuse my language."

---

* After hearing Matt mimic the call, I listened to a lot of call samples. Gibbon calls were closest to what he described.

I asked Matt if he had been in touch with his friend Andy since that visit, but he hasn't. Andy went back to Tennessee, and they fell out of contact. Any time he looked for him online, he found nothing. I tried unsuccessfully to track him down myself. If you're out there, Andy, shoot me an email. I'd love to talk to you (and Matt would too).

17

TYLER AND NATASHA

Late-Night Surprise, a Double Whammy

Ellsworth Falls, Hancock County
Late October 2006

I was put in touch with Tyler and Natasha by our mutual friend Nomar Slevik. Michael Merchant interviewed them about their astonishing run-in a few years before. I sat down and transcribed that forty-two-minute video[56] before our interview in March 2018 so that I wouldn't make them repeat themselves too much.

This is a Class A sighting from up the coast in Hancock County.

Like many Maine couples living offshore, Tyler and Natasha liked to head to the mainland and catch a movie. This was especially appealing in October. The summer traffic was gone, and winter driving conditions were distant. They were driving home well after 9:00 p.m. on US Route 1, entering Ellsworth Falls after crossing the Union River. The area was wooded, with just a few small businesses nestled in. They were both alert, keeping an eye out for deer.

They saw an orange sherbet glow ahead as they approached a lone streetlight. Natasha saw movement on the side of the road. She thought a deer was crossing, but as it moved into the road, backlit by the distant streetlight, it was clear to both of them that it was walking on two legs, not four. Tyler assumed it must be a person crossing the road. He slowed the car down considerably.

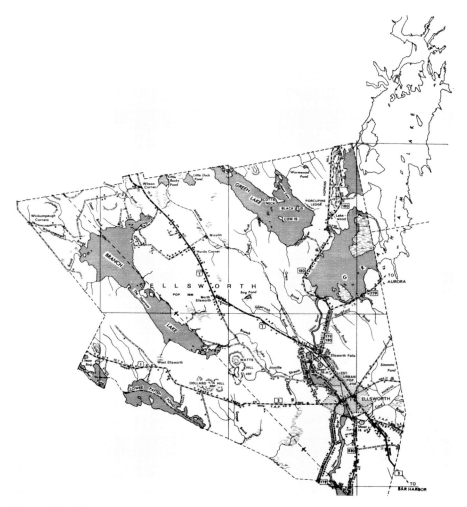

A map of the Ellsworth area. Maine General Highway Atlas, *1959.*

Its backlit form was tall and lean, more stretched out than average human height, around seven feet tall. It moved weirdly, Natasha thought, not quite like a human—maybe because its arms were too long? Tyler struggled with what he was seeing. Something odd was going on. Was someone playing a practical joke on them? The creature glanced at them and then hunched down, giving a quick look over its shoulder back the way it had come and launched itself across the remaining stretch of road on all fours. Natasha saw the way its hands scooped and curled under so it could run on its knuckles.

The motion was seamless and fluid. It was clearly born to move this way. Tyler realized this was no practical joke—it was something else entirely.

Suddenly, a smaller figure barreled across the road in front of them at high velocity. It was about half the size of what had come before and was right on its tail after a slight delay. Now they knew why the first one had looked back over its shoulder. And as quickly as that, they were gone, back into the dark woods. The entire episode only lasted a few seconds.

Tyler and Natasha were both momentarily speechless. There was no urge to stop the car, to pull over and explore. No way. That decision was unanimous.

Natasha, feeling the need to do *something*, tried to convince Tyler they should call the police. Tyler exploded in laughing disbelief. "Are you *kidding* me? What are you going to tell them?" And how would the police react? Nothing they could say would make sense. The only interruption to the silence as they continued driving home was Tyler saying decisively, "We are *never* talking about this."

And they didn't for a long, long time.

When Michael Merchant asked them their opinion of Sasquatch, it was clear they had dismissed the phenomenon before their encounter. Tyler had thought Bigfoot was mythical at best, and Natasha figured people were hoaxing the general populace, keeping the stories going. But what they saw changed their minds.

It was clear they had seen an unknown hominid. Tyler described it to Merchant as being "strangely familiar but completely alien," an "animalistic sighting…like any other wild animal you'd expect to see." Clarifying his use of the term *alien*, he added, "I don't mean like from another area, I mean strange." Natasha explained that attempting comprehension was "mindboggling and confusing. Trying to wrap your brain around what you're seeing, because it's so far outside the realm of your everyday, and what you're accustomed to seeing and knowing for the local wildlife." It was a stretch, and their brains rebelled as they tried to grapple with it.

Tyler observed that the first figure had something of an animal-in-the-headlights hesitation. "It had an arm [held] out a bit…almost hesitant. A deer would have had its neck turned [looking] out into the road before it decided what it was going to do." Natasha added, "It was almost like it froze, like we caught it, red-handed," and it was trying to figure out what to do next. In that split second, it had decided to cross the road regardless, without realizing its smaller partner wasn't following closely.

Natasha's background includes a marine biology degree and secondary science education, so she thinks in terms of classification and morphology.

She is familiar with the anatomy of a wide range of species, both marine and land based. What she saw that night ran on all fours as though "it was supposed to be moving that way." Tyler described it to Merchant: "You could see the power when they ran. So much power." The movement was noticeably different than a human. When I talked to them, they reiterated the huge power and catapulting motion of the adult and the full-tilt velocity of the smaller one.

The area they were driving through abuts a swath of forested land and a sprawling lake region. By necessity, locals are familiar with larger mammals in the area: bear, moose and deer. When pressed by Merchant about the possibility of misidentifying a bear family, Natasha responded firmly that these creatures were the wrong shape, the wrong build, the wrong morphology altogether. Bears have snouts, which these two clearly lacked. Bears don't have fingers, which these definitely had. Bears don't curl their hands under to run on their knuckles, either.

The creatures demonstrated no eyeshine in their headlights. The backlighting created a silhouette of the creature's head, shadowing its features. When I talked to them, and asked about seeing the creatures' profile, Natasha reiterated this. "I don't remember a snout. I remember feeling like I was looking at some sort of primate." Tyler agreed. The face tapered down to the jaw. I asked them about ears. Black bears have obvious ears, and both clearly stated there was no hint of ears from any angle.

The adult creature was about seven feet tall, and Tyler estimated it was over 300 pounds, comparing it to his own height of six feet and weight of 275 pounds. The creature would be heavier, since it appeared "super-muscular." Neither saw the smaller creature upright, though both thought it was around four feet tall, a miniature version of the adult. Tyler described the build of the adult as similar to a professional basketball player, larger than life like Shaquille O'Neal, no slouch at a reported seven feet and one inch, weighing 325 pounds. Tyler told Merchant, "I wouldn't say vastly out of proportion with a human other than just way long arms, and way larger. And also covered in hair, which was a big factor."

The streetlight that lit the scene was about fifty feet beyond where the pair crossed the road, backlighting them. Natasha thinks the creatures' hair was relatively uniform all over. She compared it to an orangutan: "The color of the fur on the orangutan and the length and the waviness and how it's standing straight out and the way that looks—in my memory is so similar to what we saw that night." She thinks that "it would have been hard to tell an exact color per se because the streetlight that they were backlit from had that orange tint to it." Tyler commented that the headlights could have lightened their hair. He states it was definitely not black hair, as a bear would have. Of that he is certain.

Tyler told Merchant, "I agree with her as far as uniform hair on the body. I noticed the arm sticking out before it crossed the road initially, and you could see wisps of hair.…I didn't get much sense of color on the first, but on the second, we were approaching, and the headlights definitely hit the hind end of the larger one and the passing of the smaller one, and I would say [their hair was] a little more brown than an orangutan, but…that's pretty close. Thicker, maybe, a little bit." When I talked to them both, Natasha clarified that their hair appeared substantial, as she was worried the term wispy implied thin, barely-there hair: "It was not thin."

If they hadn't driven by at that particular moment, nobody would have seen the creatures at all. They hadn't seen any other traffic there. Tyler pointed out, "It was in such a short frame of time. I don't think they were hanging around on either side of the road." It was a chance meeting, which neither party expected to occur.

Tyler commented, "I could see an arm and a hand" as the creature turned back toward the young straggler. He described it as visible body language, as "if you were waiting for somebody to come up behind you, like a child." When talking to Merchant, Natasha interpreted the quick look thrown over the shoulder, seeing the impatience of an adult toward a child when crossing any road: "Come *on*! Will you *come*? There's a *car* coming!" There weren't any visible clues about the adult's gender, but it was clearly in charge of the smaller one.

That area has been extensively developed since 2006. Nearby, forest was cleared to install a Fuddruckers and a Citgo gas station, opened in May 2015. Other businesses have expanded, installing massive roadside signage, parking and lighting alongside U.S. Route 1. Anyone who has been to Mount Desert Island knows the corridor leading up to Acadia has exploded with big box stores and multilane roadways. The landscape, especially as Route 3 peels off U.S. Route 1 toward the island, is drastically changed from ten or fifteen years ago. The built-up mallscape provides a stark contrast to the simple, quiet retreats of the region hidden beyond. However, even with this development, the surrounding land remains carpeted in forest and lake. A wilderness corridor extends north from Ellsworth as far as you can go.

Tyler and Natasha are still not Bigfoot enthusiasts but do wonder. They've pored over maps to figure out why the creatures were there. Tyler speculates that they misnavigated. He thinks that if they were heading for the coastline and accidentally headed down the southwest side of Graham Lake* instead of its eastern side, this would have dropped into Ellsworth, instead of quieter areas up the coast. Both mentioned to me that they got the impression the pair was simply traveling through.

They both still feel disbelief a dozen years later. Tyler admits, "It's crazy! It really is crazy, but like I said, it was the type of encounter where there was really no other option than to believe what you were seeing." Natasha adds, "And even then, your brain didn't *want* to believe it." The ordinariness of the circumstances was also a hurdle. As Tyler says, "It's not like I was camping up in the Allagash and had some kind of situation. We were driving home from a stupid movie." But all the same, he doesn't question what he saw. "If there was just that one animal there for a second and bolting across the road, I would've discounted it, I probably would have *never* told anybody, but to see an identical, smaller animal, creature or whatever you want to call it run by—that just cemented it in our mind.... We know exactly what we saw. It was so cut and dry."

At one point, Natasha attended a local talk by Daniel C. Taylor, author of *Yeti: The Ecology of a Myth* (Oxford University Press, 2017). "I felt so uncomfortable with what I saw that I wanted someone to prove me wrong. I wanted to find someone who could say, 'Oh, no, you didn't see that, silly. *This* is what you saw' and to have it make sense, because the traditional paradigm of animals that we're familiar with in this area did not fit with that sighting at all. And to me, that causes a lot of mental conflict. I don't like the gray area—I like black and white."

She went, drawn by her background in science education, interested to hear how Taylor developed his theory that the legendary yeti is actually the Himalayan brown bear. She lingered after the presentation to talk to him and was rebuffed when he laughed her off, telling her, "Of course it was a bear." He did so without demonstrating a logical path to that answer. "There was no correlation between what he was saying and the observations we had made." He dismissed their observations. She left disappointed.

Until they talked to Michael Merchant, "It was just a story that we felt served no purpose," Tyler admitted. "I had told somebody the story where I work....I guess he had another friend who was highly into [Bigfoot], and he mentioned the story to him, and then that's how Mike found out." They

---

* Graham Lake is a thirteen-mile-long manmade reservoir lake just north of Ellsworth.
"Graham Lake (Maine)," Wikipedia, last edited May 6, 2017, en.wikipedia.org.

told me they want their encounter on record, available for anyone who can make use of it—the same reason they let Merchant interview them. Tyler explained, "I really don't feel like the sighting serves me any great purpose, because nobody will believe it unless they see it themselves. And I can understand that. I would have rather seen my favorite celebrity or something, maybe." He laughed at the absurdity of it all. "I would have rather had somebody like you have the sighting, who would know what to do. Unlike us, 'Whoa, we're out of here!'" To which, Natasha interjected, "Well, you were—I wanted to call somebody!"

Regardless, Tyler says, "I would like to have it documented somehow, some way, somewhere."

Natasha avers that she still has no desire to go camping (which is nothing new), and Tyler, while surprised no one has discovered a specimen for identification yet, is sure their encounter was "a very rare occurrence….I never get worried about camping and hunting and fishing because I just don't think [it was anything but luck]. We just happened to go by at the right moment."

18

JEFF KAINE

How to Stampede a Fisherman

Moro Plantation, Aroostook County
Late May 2007

I almost overlooked Jeff's email, since he wrote it in a short story format, and thus I misinterpreted it as creative fiction writing. In reviewing it a couple years later, I realized it rang too true. I emailed Jeff to clear this up, and he stated unequivocally that it was written from his own experience and not fictionalized.

This is a Class B encounter from Aroostook County. In spite of having no visuals to report, I think you will agree it is memorable.

Jeff was celebrating a day off with a fishing trip to Green Pond. The little sixteen-acre pond, well stocked with good-sized trout, was in the middle of nowhere and his current favorite. He had fished there over a dozen times in the last few years. Today was perfect—very little wind and a bright blue sky. The warmth of the sun quickly eliminated any chill left over from the Aroostook spring night, chasing it from the shadows as they shrank.

Leaving his truck behind, he navigated the increasingly swampy trail. Once at the pond, there was one last bit of tricky business before getting to the fun—you had to get your flippers on over your waders and boots and out of the shore muck and into your float tube. Once these tribulations were surmounted, you could enjoy the rest of the day. The pond was glass, and trout rose, leaving telltale dimples here and there on the surface of the water.

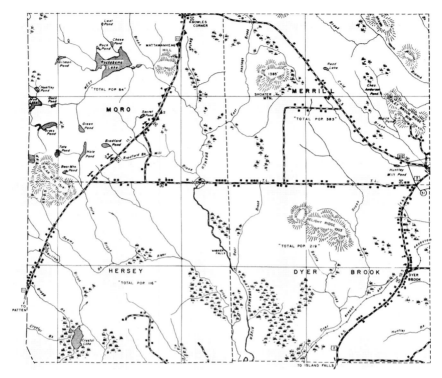

A map of both Moro Plantation and the Mattawamkeag area. Maine General Highway Atlas, *1959*.

At eleven o'clock in the morning, hours of doing nothing much stretched before him, a pleasant prospect for any fisherman.

A couple of hours passed in quiet reverie. This golden silence was interrupted by two loud knocks that rang out halfway up a wooded ridge on the opposite shoreline. Jeff didn't think much of it. The Maine woods are full of all sorts of noises. It was an odd sound, like someone swinging a baseball bat against a tree twice, but not odd enough to disrupt his enjoyable afternoon for an investigation. Quiet was restored as the echoes died out. Another couple of hours meandered by.

The stillness was broken by the crack of a large branch or small tree being snapped in half at the bottom of the wooded ridge close to the shore. Again, quiet returned, until an hour later, when a single loud knock sounded from the side of the pond where Jeff was fishing from his float. It sounded like it came from the dirt road leading to the pond. It did not occur to him that something was circling him, and he remained unfazed, caught in his fishing reverie. Eventually, only an hour of sunlight remained. The fish were popping up in anticipation of dinner, taking advantage of the last warm water as the sun slipped down. This was the usual happy payoff for a Maine spring day of slow fishing, and he was in the right place at the right time—or so he thought. Someone else felt differently.

Just after 7:00 p.m., out of the previously calm evening air, a giant roar came ripping toward him from the direction of his truck. It was a deep, angry noise that carried across the water and went right through him where he sat, frozen in his float tube. The roar went on for about five seconds, long enough for all the hair on his body to stand up of its own accord. As soon as it stopped, Jeff set off at full speed for the shore landing, wanting more than anything to get to his truck. It didn't even matter that the sound seemed to have come from near where he parked. The truck was his only escape route, and he was going to get there in record time.

Once he hit the shore, he didn't stop to take off his flippers. He hopped out of the pond and skimmed across the mucky area with his flippers still on over his boots, making a crazy run up the hill that led to his truck and safety. He hurled the float tube in back, chucked the flippers in with it and once his rod landed safely with them, he drove off without a backward glance, still in his boots and waders. Nothing was going to stop him from getting out of there. Almost half an hour later, he pulled to a stop in Patten long enough to yank off his waders and make sure his fishing gear was properly stowed before the long drive home to central Maine.

On the way home, Jeff usually pondered the fish caught and lost, scheming future improvements on that ratio. This time, those pleasant thoughts were forestalled by his brain replaying the events of the day. "That's why I remember so much of the odd details," he said. "Riding home, I had time to think of those two wood knocks high up on that ridge—knocks that echoed across the pond like I was in an amphitheater. And that branch or tree snapping in half. The third wood knock and of course the roaring sound that scared the bejesus out of me. Everything was being played over and over for the entire two-hour drive home because I was freaked the hell out."

He drew a mental map of the events. "The noises I had been hearing throughout the day did a complete circle around me. Starting up on that ridge in the early afternoon and going counterclockwise around the pond, until ending up to within maybe fifty yards of my truck." He was also preoccupied with the roar. "I have heard all kinds of different animal noises while fishing the woods of Maine. I've heard owls, moose, deer, birds of all species, coyotes, loons hissing, raccoons growling and dogs barking. I've heard coyotes killing their prey." What he hadn't heard in real life, he knew from watching documentaries, including black bear growls. Except for that roar: "I've never heard any animal sound like this before, and no human could ever replicate what I heard that evening in late May, so what was it?"

He told his family, but they passed it off as a fisherman's tall tale. But it wasn't anything of the sort. Over ten years later, he was still in exile from his favorite fishing spot, which he had vowed to fish every year for the rest of his life. He didn't mention his encounter again until a few years ago, hanging out with an old friend while he worked on Jeff's truck. The garage owner grew up less than a mile from Jeff and fished that same pond with him on more than one occasion. It was only natural for Jeff to confide in him.

"I started to tell him, and by the look on his face, I immediately knew I had finally found somebody that believed my tale. And this wasn't the kind of look where he just looked interested in what I was saying. He had a look that told me he had something to say as well." Once Jeff finished, his friend related his own encounter from a year after Jeff's. He was fishing that same pond and heard that same roar, which he described as being "so deep that his insides shook." Jeff's fishing companion continued to fish the pond occasionally but was leery of going alone.

With this corroboration, Jeff felt more comfortable telling another friend, an interested skeptic. Not long after, the friend got back in touch. He had a friend with a camp near Green Pond. He'd asked him about anything strange in the area. This camp owner had a friend who "was fishing the same pond, when several rocks started flying out of the woods and landing in the water all around him. He thought it might be [the camp owner] playing a joke on him, but [the camp owner] was home that weekend, thus it wasn't him. He also said based on the size of the rocks and the distance they were being thrown it seemed unlikely a person would be able to do that." Jeff put me in touch with the friend, and he confirmed this account.

In terms of human interference, Jeff notes that due to the layout of the dirt road, you can hear any vehicle approaching the pond, and the remoteness of the location precludes chance human encounters. As he says, "So where did the rocks come from? Who was throwing them?"

Green Pond is located just over a mile from the Aroostook Scenic Highway (Route 11) as the crow flies. The surrounding area is mostly boggy or wooded (or both), though much of the forest has been thinned by partial harvesting of the lumber in recent years, clearly visible in Google Maps aerial shots. Nearby Moro Plantation had only thirty-eight residents according to the 2010 U.S. Census. Green Pond is directly to the east of Baxter State Park.

19

JEFF ROBERTSON

Disappearing Rocks and Nocturnal Bandits

L‌IVERMORE F‌ALLS AND A‌NDROSCOGGIN R‌IVER A‌REA, A‌NDROSCOGGIN C‌OUNTY
A‌PRIL 2011 O‌NWARD

This account returns us to Androscoggin River waterways and includes a sighting in Leeds, a known Maine nexus for odd sightings. I spoke to both Jeff and his son Seth about these intriguing events, which ended around 2017–18 due to forest clearance.

These are a mix of Class A and Class B sightings.

A‌ROUND THE SPRING OF 2011, Jeff Robertson and his son Seth were fiddleheading near the brook behind Jeff's house. When Seth said, "Hey, Dad, come check this out!" Jeff retraced his steps. Seth pointed out a huge footprint on the muddy path. Jeff had stepped right into it without even noticing.

"*No way,*" Jeff said, staring at it. "No way!" It looked like a perfect human footprint but dwarfed Jeff's size twelve boot. Seth snapped a picture. There were other footprints nearby, but that was the clearest one, showing a set of toes. There were no claw marks, just the big toe and the four smaller toes lined up next to it.

Jeff began noticing other things. He heard a funny "Whooooo," which was answered by three tree-knocks from behind a neighbor's house. Mysterious noises came from the summer woods behind his home. Between

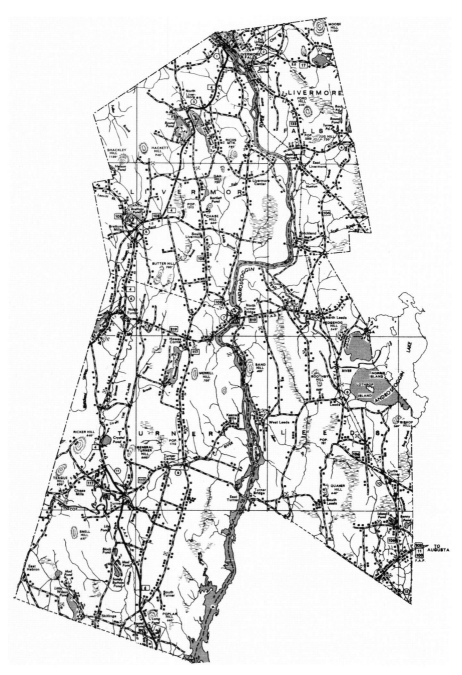

A map of the Livermore Falls, Turner and Leeds area. Maine General Highway Atlas, *1959.*

2:00 and 3:00 a.m., large branches were broken, trees shaken, tree-knocks echoed and vocalizations occurred unlike any he knew from years spent outdoors. This reoccurred every couple of weeks. Was something moving through the area periodically?

Jeff's birdfeeder was broken numerous times. The first time he discovered it empty on the ground, he picked it up and fixed it. It happened again. He fixed it once more. The third time, he was awake, smoking at an open window and watching the sky lighten through the woods. Just for fun he let out a "WhooooOOOOOoooo" in imitation of the Bigfoot calls he'd heard on *Finding Bigfoot*. The results were astonishing. Startled by the noise, his birdfeeder culprit took off across the lawn on two legs, crossing no more than twelve feet in front of the window where Jeff stood. "I was going to scream out the window, 'Hey what are you doing?' but the words wouldn't come out of my mouth; I was just that scared."

The figure was about six feet tall and covered in black hair. As it ran by, it stared in blind panic back at where Jeff was hidden in the shadows behind his window screen. Then it disappeared into the woods. It had dark eyes and kind of a squashed nose, without much hair on its face. Jeff was in a state of shock, the hair on the back of his neck electrified. I forgot to ask him if he fixed the birdfeeder again after that.

Jeff's other notable encounter was about ten miles from his home when he was out running errands one summer day. Driving across the Androscoggin River bridge on Route 219, just past the Twin Bridge Market in Leeds, he noticed two big black boulders a few feet offshore in the river below, one larger than the other. The second time he went by, the "boulders" were in different locations. Hmm, not boulders then. They weren't moving much but just sitting in the water. Were they fishing? For what? When he drove back from Lewiston, they were gone.

He speculated whether it was the same family behind his home. He knew they weren't the boulders they had first appeared to be. The river was at a low ebb, and even at full bore, it wouldn't move boulders *that* big. As he said with great certainty, "No, boulders don't move like that….Boulders that big don't disappear." As you cross the bridge, there are falls just below. Then the river sweeps around a left-hand corner and widens out a bit. It was in this section that the two creatures were sitting. He still checks that spot every time he drives by, just in case they're out fishing again.

Over the years, Jeff has written notes of his experiences, including hundreds of tree-knocks. He is partly convinced they signal different meanings, depending on their combinations. Sometimes he goes out behind his house when he's up at 2:00 or 3:00 a.m. to try his hand at it from a safe distance. "I can make them answer back. I'm not going [to go] in the woods, but I can make them answer me back." I asked him if he'd talked to any neighbors. "There's a few, but they don't really want to talk about it." Folks are perfectly comfortable talking about coydogs, foxes, bobcats and other average Maine wildlife traversing their backyards, but anything beyond that results in ridicule. When I interviewed his son Seth several months later, he was willing to answer my questions about the footprints he found with his dad but added, "He's the one that's more interested in that stuff than I am."

Seth is a hunter and is in the woods all the time. He pays attention to his surroundings, which is why he noticed the track his dad stepped in. "I was walking along, and he was in front of me. He ended up actually stepping right in the track, and that's when I ended up seeing it." He agrees that it was a singular experience. "I've never really seen anything like that before. It was definitely unique." I asked him where they found the track, and he described the range of the land, from where the house sits a long way above the brook down into the valley. As the land starts to rise on the other side of the brook, it breaks into farmers' fields, mostly haying. The tree growth, predominantly mature pine, was recently logged, opening it up noticeably.

His dad thought they'd lost the photo of the footprint, but Seth still had it. Over the years, Seth had backed up his old flip phone onto his computer. He had rediscovered the footprint photo and loaded it onto his current phone. Clearly, the occasion still stood out in his mind, even several years later. I asked him if other footprints were visible nearby, and he said, "I found a few of them, but only one was significant, so you could actually tell it was a foot with toes." He noted the toes are visible in the photo, although the quality is not great, since it was an earlier cellphone model. "But you can see it, for the most part, pretty clearly. You can see his boot print right inside it, actually." He verified that there were no claws or other indications that the print was from a bear and described seeing all five toes in the mud. The print, he said "was substantially bigger [than the boot print]. It probably goes another three inches past the back of his boot. He stepped up by the toes."

This footprint and Jeff's experiences make an interesting mélange. As we finished talking on the phone that night in May 2018, Jeff added a little bit of historical flavor to the scene. "When I was little, I used to live in Monmouth, and it was considered the Leeds Devil. I'm pretty sure I encountered him

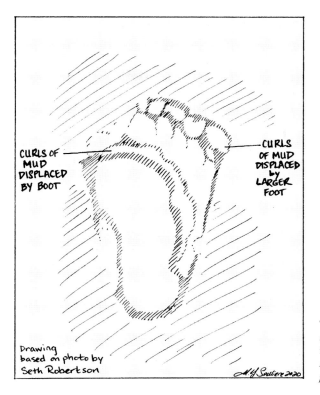

CURLS OF
MUD
DISPLACED
BY BOOT

CURLS
OF MUD
DISPLACED
by
LARGER
FOOT

Drawing
based on photo by
Seth Robertson

The footprint found by Jeff and Seth Robertson while fiddleheading. *Illustration by Michelle Y. Souliere, based on photo by Seth Robertson.*

over that way, but you know, we didn't actually see him. It was me and a few of my buddies, and it was like, 'Oh my God, let's get the hell out!' Of course, we were young, you know. Fifteen, sixteen years old." They had heard tree-knocks and howls. Leeds is about fifteen miles south of where Jeff lives now. "I'm going to be honest," he added, reflecting on his experiences, "if I hadn't seen it, I still wouldn't believe it."

Jeff continues to keep an eye on the woods but is protective of his grandchildren: "I won't let my kids down back in the dark, *at all.*"

20

ROGER LANE

Strange Tracks and Stranger Sounds

Baileyville, St. Croix River Valley, Washington County
Autumn 2011 Onward

This is another case where small details add up. It is my only report from the easternmost part of Maine, where the state butts up underneath New Brunswick, Canada, which has plenty of Bigfoot sightings of its own.

This is a Class B sighting from Washington County. Sounds were heard and potential tracks were seen, but the lack of additional information leaves room for misinterpretation or misidentification.

The bridge between September and October often gifts Mainers with a stretch of beautiful weather, a last reassurance of perfectly warm days before the deep chill of late fall sets in. Roger Lane stepped onto his porch at about 2:00 a.m. to have a smoke outdoors. It was unusually warm. Suddenly, out of the peace and quiet erupted a terrifyingly loud growl. It permeated his entire body, right down to the bones, vibrating his insides. Peculiarly, alongside the growl came a high-pitched noise. This went on for at least half a minute, emerging from the river corridor wilderness, not far from Roger's doorstep at the edge of tiny Baileyville.

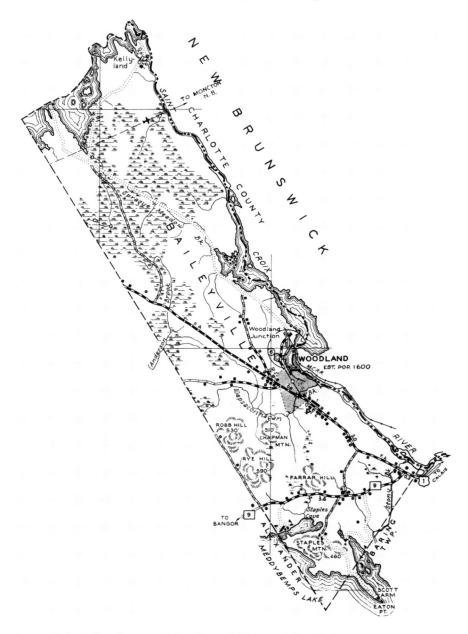

A map of the Baileyville area. Maine General Highway Atlas, *1959.*

As it stopped, he hopped back inside and snapped on his police scanner. At that volume, the noise must have woken the whole town. But there was nothing. He was floored.*

Later that year, in December 2011, he was out hunting with his beagles before daybreak. He liked to head out early so the dogs would be tired before dark, making it easier to round them up. Fresh snow had fallen overnight, leaving a couple of inches for easy tracking. A few flakes trickled down as he opened the truck door and let the dogs out. The sunrise lightened the sky in the east as he followed the dogs up the hill. They sniffed the tree line spots where they knew the rabbits came in and out. He hoped to angle them toward the easier trail, but as usual, they were more interested in where the hill dropped into a thicket, making it impossible for him to get a shot in even if they did jump a rabbit.

He waited on the path, listening for their barks. Ahead of him on the slope, he saw footprints in the snow. It struck him as odd that somebody beside himself would have been out so early. The tracks went up the road before cutting into the woods. The dogs hadn't found anything exciting yet, so he took a closer look.

The tracks appeared to be human. Roger's own footprints were a little larger than his size twelve foot. These tracks were easily as big. Then he noticed a smaller set of tracks accompanying the first, half that size. He reached inside the larger tracks to see if he could feel impressions from toes or boot treads, but sticky snow had blown into the tracks, obscuring any details. He wished he could brush it out of the tracks to identify them. He guessed they were from 1:00 or 2:00 a.m., a few hours before his arrival.

Why was somebody out here in a snowstorm at that time of night, and why cut into the woods instead of walking down the main dirt road? Were they intentionally staying out of sight from the main road? None of it made sense. Either way, it didn't sit well with him to hunt his dogs in that area not knowing what was in the woods with them. It wasn't worth the risk.

He rounded up the dogs and stayed away from that area on future hunting trips. He went back later to see where the tracks started, and they emerged onto the dirt road from a smaller side road. He followed them to a little creek that fed into the St. Croix River. He remained baffled.

When I interviewed him, Roger tried to describe the peculiar two-tone growl he heard on that first night. It was a tandem tone, one a growl with

---

* Roger would hear that same growl a number of times over the next several years while out wildlife watching near the natural gas pipeline. The pipeline's cut-throughs and sideroads provide locals with some great lookouts.

tremendous bass, much akin to a male lion's territorial roar, which can be heard from up to five miles (eight kilometers) away.[57] It was steady, and he said, "I could feel my insides shaking from the bassy-ness of it." Alongside the growl was a high-pitched noise he compared in tone to the pitch of "a pack of young coyotes going off crazily. They'll do it a lot if they're running rabbit…if they're at a kill site. The high-pitched barking that they make was just about the right pitch, I would say."

Roger Lane has been a hunter all his life. In the years since the event, he has asked others if they've encountered anything similar. "If they're hunters, and if they've sat down at my table or I've sat down at theirs for fifteen or twenty minutes, I've talked to them about it." The upshot? People are unwilling to speak about things like this. "I think a lot of people care too much what other people think, and quite frankly, I really don't care." He chuckled as he said this, and I did too. What a different world it would be if people worried less about ridicule over personal experiences.

"I know what I've heard. I know what I've seen. Um…can I say it's Bigfoot? Nope, I can't. I don't know exactly what it is….But there's something out there. Like I said, I hunt with some of the biggest guns that people put on their shoulders, and I'm not so sure that I ever want to come nose-to-nose with it." In a later conversation, he elaborated further. "I learned to trap at a very young age and spent many winter nights in the woods on old beaver flowages. I'd been taught that there's nothing to fear that walks in the woods but to rather be leery of man. I'm not so sure that this is the case now. I do not fear the woods but have little doubt that I don't want to bump into whatever it is, armed or not."

He still goes out hunting, and if he treads a little more carefully, he doesn't let his encounters stop him. "It's made me a little bit more aware. Put it that way. It's not that I'm afraid of it. Having been deployed so many times, I've come to grips with [the fact] that we're all going to die at some point of time in our lives, and nobody's going to escape it….It made me just a little more aware that there may be things out there that I don't *know* exist or that a lot of people haven't seen."

21

DAN SOUCY

Noisy Shadows at Sunset

Brunswick/Durham Area, Cumberland and Androscoggin Counties
October 2013 Onward

I've talked with Dan for over a decade now. We both love Maine folklore, and I recommend his books to anyone interested in Maine's lesser-known stories. For years, Dan has tromped through the woods quietly exploring and occasionally sharing his thoughts via YouTube.[58] His most striking encounter occurred not far from Portland, near the Androscoggin River in the Brunswick/Durham area. Dan spoke about his encounters at the 2015 *Finding Bigfoot* town hall meeting. I followed up with him in early 2019.

This is a Class B sighting. Lighting conditions and undergrowth obscured a full view, although the accompanying sounds and chain of events add spice.

After spotting a pile of neatly stacked shells on the riverbank in 2008 while out fiddleheading, Dan continued finding tracks and other interesting traces of activity in an area he particularly liked to hike. Today he'd found some really different scat, full of fur and remnants of meat, with an unusual texture. He'd examined the surrounding area thoroughly, and the sun was setting when he headed home. He hadn't planned to be out this late and didn't have his flashlights or headlamp with him.

To his left, he heard something walking through the brush. The substantial noise made him pay attention. It could be anything, including a bear, although he hadn't seen bear signs for years. It was getting darker, the light fading above as the sun dropped behind the slope.

He heard larger and larger sticks being broken. With a quickening heartbeat, he heard noises from the undergrowth ahead. Past tracks he'd found indicated four different individuals frequented the area. How many were with him tonight? The increasing twilight obscured Dan's view. He heard whistles from ahead and behind. They came in short sharp bursts, the kind of whistle used to inform someone of location. Beyond a small infrared light (IR), he wasn't equipped for low-light filming, The IR light cast a small radius of illumination, and the creatures were keeping well back. He couldn't get a clear view of his mysterious traveling companions, just hints of their tall forms dashing through the woods around him.

He continued on, not knowing what might happen next. Something large and bulky moved through the woods on his right, heading over the backlit slope of the ridge. A few shadowy forms flicked past the glare of the dying sunset, slipping between trees. He heard large tree limbs being broken, a heavy, distinct sound different from something pushing through twigs and brush. But after a flurry of accelerated activity, things quieted down. Although clearly interested in him, they didn't bother to follow him farther as he headed over the ridge toward the roadway, preferring their own nocturnal pursuits. Dan walked home with a lot to think about.

Dan described this as hands-down "the most intense moment" of his investigatory career. He was surrounded and outnumbered. Dan is not excitable, describing himself as "rather stoic." He has a straightforward and pragmatic approach. That evening, "there was a heightened adrenaline level and greater sensory perception." Everything was sharp and clear, moment by moment, and he had been ready for anything to happen.

Dan talks to other investigators in the area, comparing notes and developing theories. One theory is that the population, in solitude or compact family groups, works through a large loop spanning many miles, which takes about thirty or forty days to traverse. As he says, "We've found if we're in certain areas at certain times, you can go back within that thirty- to forty-day timeframe, and you'll find new sign." It makes sense if you don't want to exhaust slow-growing flora, taking advantage of seasonal changes for different food types. Black bears in Maine use similar practices.

When the *Finding Bigfoot* crew was in Maine, they spent time with Dan, which wasn't seen in the episode, arriving late because of flight delays. Viewers will note the team did nighttime filming at Bradbury Mountain State Park, not far as the crow flies from Brunswick and the Androscoggin River.

In the past, Dan's fieldwork was limited by his job, but he looks forward to spending more time in the woods since retirement. "It's kind of too bad," he told me. "I think I missed out on some significant findings…a lot more evidence than I have, as far as developing a reliable line of investigation." Dan's goal? "Simply to find them. Get definitive proof." Whether it's DNA evidence or impeccable photographic or video evidence, it must be solid enough to withstand a barrage of scrutiny. Out on the trails, he keeps his camera running. He carries it on a tripod, with the camera looking ahead from about a foot and a half off the ground, to document tracks he might need to doublecheck later.

Dan is understandably reticent about pinpointing locations after losing active sites to additional human presence, a common worry of investigators. He stopped mentioning specific locations in his YouTube videos to prevent further interference. "Some of the places I've been at have been totally trashed and changed." Some sites were overrun by off-road vehicle activity, others were obliterated by recent construction. Luckily, Maine is big. Even with rapid development in southern Maine, in some areas, man and beast can roam freely between the trees. Here's hoping freedom of movement continues to be the norm in the woods of Maine.

22

KATHY

It Made No Effort to Run or Hide

Berwick, York County
Late May 2016

This is a brief sighting in broad daylight that rattles the eyewitness to this day. I heard about it from her daughter, and six months later, I finally established contact with the eyewitness herself. While she hoped the information would be helpful to my readers, she didn't want to discuss it more than necessary. I am very grateful that she talked to me because this case provides an interesting link with Lynne Collett's sighting from forty years earlier, less than three miles away as the crow flies.

This is a Class A sighting, another from York County, close to the New Hampshire border.

It was early morning, about 6:30 a.m., when Kathy and her husband drove away from her daughter's camp. As they headed back toward civilization, they crossed a small bridge. Kathy looked out her passenger-side window as they passed over the water and saw a big dark figure turn slowly and watch their car go by.

She stared at its long, low-hanging arms as it stood straight up from a crouch. She avoided making eye contact. It was taller than a man with wide shoulders, and it did not move as it watched their car drive by above the small slope. It was covered in black matted hair, "not that red brown you

Above: The bridge in Berwick near Kathy's sighting location. *Photo by Michelle Y. Souliere.*

Opposite: A typical back road in Berwick, near Kathy's sighting location. *Photo by Michelle Y. Souliere.*

hear about from the TV shows," and it had huge hands. "It didn't make an effort to run or hide, which I think scared me the most," Kathy told me. "I really try not to think about it, and I have not been back up that way since."

Kathy had watched episodes of *Finding Bigfoot* but never thought they were actually hunting for a real creature. She thought Bigfoot was something people imagined they saw when they misidentified an existing animal. "I do know now that what I saw was not something else. It scared me to death. I could not speak." She was so terrified that she didn't even get her husband's attention or talk to him about it later on their ride home, "for fear he would stop the car and want to go look." Besides, "no one I ever came in contact with ever talked about a Bigfoot sighting. No one would believe you anyway or [they would] think you were a little off."

In November 2018, I went with a friend to visit the area. The soil near the bridge is tawny sand, covered in dry pine tassels. The surrounding forest is a mix of very old and very young trees, like much of southern Maine, including softwoods and hardwoods, oaks and evergreens. The small river

chatters loudly as it slips under the mossy bridge and then quietly heads downstream on the other side, running between wooded banks.

Paradise is not without trouble. There are obvious traces of litter from partying and illegal dumping at the side of the river. The local sheriff keeps a close eye on nearby camps during winter due to regular vandalism. Many areas are clearly marked "NO TRESPASSING," so we didn't explore beyond the small bridge. While there, we saw two carloads of greasepainted young hunters heading out, so we were glad we had our blaze orange hats. On nearby dirt roads, we found similar environments, riddled with streams, ponds and boggy areas. The ruddy hint of autumn blueberry barrens lay across recently cleared areas. The dark wet bark of bare shrubs contrasted with the orangey dampness of the sandy topsoil. Forested areas were dense with ground cover where the ground wasn't too swampy.

Kathy still hasn't been back to the area and isn't interested in returning any time soon.

23

DAVE

Surprise Family Visit and Other Encounters

Near the Saco River Basin, York County
April 2017

This case has been challenging to write about. It involves multiple locations, witnesses and encounters, and the eyewitness worries that human interference will drive the family group to relocate, so I tread carefully in describing it.

This is a Class A sighting, with multiple eyewitnesses, from York County. It starts out mildly but by the end becomes quite extraordinary.

For a couple of years, Dave had happily hiked a wilderness preserve near his home, about twenty miles from Portland. A regular birdwatcher, he found that there were always new things to see. It wasn't until he encountered footprints in February 2016 that he thought there might be something else in the woods. The footprints were in snow near a well-traveled trail. The clearest six to eight footprints showed toe marks. The tracks were slightly over twelve inches in length.

When shown photos, even skeptical relatives admitted they were intrigued. Dave decided to start keeping his eyes out, and not just for birds. He wasn't sure what else to do. After several months, he submitted the photos to the BFRO. He was contacted by Jeff, an investigator here in New England. In August 2016, Jeff traveled to Maine to meet Dave and see the location.

Please stay on marked trails! A common sight and good advice on Maine's better trail systems. *Photo by Michelle Y. Souliere.*

He showed Dave how to identify what might or might not be clues and described the hallmarks of the large visitors they were looking for. On that first expedition, they heard an odd whoofing noise and the sound of something following alongside them in the woods.

Jeff's purpose in visiting was twofold. Less than five miles away, a couple of kids reported they were fishing in a small pond when they were scared off by a Bigfoot. The two men went to check out the second site together, and Dave returned there many times afterward and found large tracks (around seventeen inches long). A month after his first visit, Dave encountered a massive tree structure he believes was not manmade. Several trees, most quite large, were leaned into each other, creating a teepee-style conical shape, one large tree positioned with its root ball uppermost. The structure hadn't been there on his first visit with Jeff. Two months later, Dave scanned past a swampy area with his binoculars and spotted a large, black, hairy shape. At first, he thought it might be a bear. After twenty minutes, it still hadn't moved. Open lowland instead of a tree or hidden nook seemed an odd place for a bear to nap, although not completely unheard of. Maybe it was a weird stump? The next weekend when he returned, it had disappeared. It was definitely not a stump.

In April 2017, Jeff returned with Kate, a fellow Bigfooter. Starting at the second location, they examined the tree structure Dave reported and found tracks near the swamp. They headed over to Dave's original location. There was heavy cloud cover, and it started to rain, but Dave convinced them to check what he felt was a family gathering spot, where a half dozen or more young birch trees had been laid at right angles, creating an open-ended "room." Slipping in mud on the hilly trail, they made their way with flashlights in the chilly April evening. Dave scoured the woods with his flashlight in search of the familiar white-bark formation. What he saw instead still seems unbelievable.

"Oh my god…I see *eyes*!" Dave exclaimed. Jeff urged everyone to turn off their flashlights. A mere stone's throw into the woods to the left of the trail, they could see eyes glowing out of the dark from varying heights. Dave recalls hearing his companions counting aloud beside him: "'There's one set of eyes, there's two, there's three.' They got up to six." The dark forms from which they emanated were only a couple dozen feet from them, Dave estimates. Two of the six were taller, the other four much closer to the ground. Dave assumed these were juveniles.

Of the juveniles, Kate noticed one set of eyes glowed emerald green, two sets glowed white and one glowed an intense red orange. The taller ones both glowed white, according to Kate. Dave observed that the eyes were widely set, about four inches apart on each face. At one point, a juvenile's eyes glowed so brightly that both Kate and Dave were able to see its face. She described it as a large black ape face. Dave could clearly see darker iris lines radiating out from their pupils. The creatures swayed restlessly, except for one of the taller ones, which froze in place, watching. The juveniles on each end would squat lower and then stand back up again, while the two in the middle appeared less agitated. In the moment, the hikers didn't think of leaving as they watched the glowing eyes and dark forms in the twilight. Kate estimated that they stood there a good six to eight minutes, though to Dave it felt more like twenty.

Suddenly, they heard a loud, full-lunged howl. It was nearby in the woods. The creatures did not reply. Dave, Jeff and Kate moved closer to see better, knowing a photograph in the rain would be useless—a blurry mess no one would ever believe. As soon as they stepped forward, they heard a deep, resonating growl from one of the taller pair, shocking in its realness. This was not imaginary; these were actual animals. Another growl came. It was clearly time to go, whether the growl was warning the curious juveniles to stay put or warning the humans away. So, the humans said their farewells and departed from the shining eyes and down the slippery mud track, half-frozen, soaking wet, jittery with shock and stunned into silence. Another growl from the tree line rattled their ribcages and hastened their steps.

Eventually, they turned on their lights again. They were accompanied by the intense feeling of being followed. As they emerged from the tree line and set off down the last stretch of open trail toward their vehicles, Kate was startled by a pair of glowing green eyes blinking from the left just off the road. Dave turned, and his flashlight illuminated the creature's matted hair before he quickly directed the light back toward the ground to avoid upsetting it. He couldn't help wishing he could signal it somehow. Jeff discouraged him from flashing the light at it further, and they continued on, leaving the creature to its solitary watch and wondering about all they had seen.

I interviewed Dave first. After hearing his story, I contacted Jeff and Kate independently. Each related their own version of the events. It is a fascinating and singular account shared jointly between three adventurous people.

After the excitement of that evening, Dave waited a couple of weeks before going back, not wanting to scare them away—typical of his caution. He doesn't carry plaster to cast tracks with. He doesn't carry a camera with him beyond his cellphone, which he keeps tucked away most of the time. But he did take a moment on his first return trip to check the area where the last vigilant creature stood to watch them go and found signs that something large had disrupted the undergrowth where it emerged and stood. He hiked in to where they encountered the family, and "it looked to me like they'd dismantled a little bit of it. And that kind of made me feel bad."

He continues to occasionally find tracks and hear tree-knocks. He camped at the second location for a couple of nights in August 2017. A thunderstorm blew through, and he almost lost his tent. Somehow, he managed to get to sleep, only to wake later, storm long gone, to footsteps crunching in a circle around his tent. "Of course," he said, "I always think bears, because I'm scared to death of bears. I think in a past life I was eaten by a bear or something." But it might be one of the local Bigfoots. With a surge of extreme worry, it occurred to him, "What if they *don't* accept me? What do I do if he starts throwing rocks at me?" The footsteps crunched around him for maybe ten or fifteen minutes as he lay there, frozen. And then it left. In the morning, he found plenty of broken undergrowth but no tracks.

A solitary watch along the trail, keeping track of the humans. *Illustration by Michelle Y. Souliere.*

In my visits to these locations, I have gotten a feel for them and seen all of their seasonal colors. The two locations are similar in their mixture of birch and alder trees and pines, as well as substantial undergrowth. The trails are well maintained but not heavily traveled. In the first location, the trails move hikers through a wide variety of rolling and flat terrain, both wooded areas and low-growth, partially cleared areas, while the second is mostly steep ridges.

Both locations have residences adjoining them and roads around them, but in neither case are the homes and businesses prolific in activity. Both have ample water sources, the first with many brooks and streams, the second with a pond and adjoining swampy area. The first location has diverse populations of deer, turkey, grouse, coyote, hares and many small mammals. The second location seems to have less animal life, perhaps because it is smaller and hemmed in by residences. In both locations, undergrowth and ridges throughout the forested areas provide cover for animals to move through invisibly, even when trees are bare.

Dave continues to visit both locations in all seasons, and whether or not he encounters anything like he did that gloomy April night, he relishes every chance to get out in the woods and explore some of Maine's best open-air treasures.

PART III

ADDITIONAL CONTEXT, CURIOSITIES AND CONCLUSIONS

24

MAINE BIGFOOT INVESTIGATORS

The most visible element in modern-day cryptozoology is the group of people who choose to publicly announce their involvement in the field. Maine is no different.

Some investigators opt to focus on historic and folkloric research, performing solo fieldwork quietly when opportunity allows. Some feel compelled to publish, whether through YouTube, Facebook or in print. Many start out alone but might join groups eventually, whether pre-existing or self-made. I believe that the majority of Maine Bigfoot investigators will never be known by the public at large and are happy to remain anonymous.

This chapter will shine a brief light on a few people visibly working in the field and their views on Bigfoot in Maine.

Dan Soucy is a hardworking author whose books can be found in print at Lulu.com or through The History Press. He is easy to contact online via one of his blogs[59] or his YouTube channel.[60] He spends more time outdoors now that he's retired and is a longtime researcher of Maine history, folklore and woodsmanship. You can read about his personal experiences in the eyewitness section of this book.

Michael Merchant is nothing if not visible. He began posting YouTube videos[61] early in 2011 and is still going strong. Most Bigfoot fans will know him as a contestant, along with fellow Mainer Kat McKechnie (Maine Ghost Hunters), on *Ten Million Dollar Bigfoot Bounty*, which aired its first and only season early in 2014 on Spike Network. For years, Merchant has generously shared his interviews of Maine eyewitnesses, for which we are indebted to him. He has added encounters of his own in recent years.

Bill Brock is another highly visible investigator, running the gamut across all categories of the unexplained. He is best known for his show *Monsters Underground* on Destination America, which premiered in 2014, and his 2017 *Rogue Mysteries* series and the UFO documentary short film *Abducted New England* (2018). He released a trailer for *Sasquatch New England* late in the summer of 2018, but the production has yet to be released.[62]

Chris Julian founded the Bigfoot Research Group of the Northeast (later renamed Maine Bigfoot Research) in the early 1990s. He placed ads in the *Track Record*, a long-running Bigfoot publication by Ray Crowe, seeking local eyewitnesses. A decade into his work, he started a Yahoo group.[63] In December 2008, he dropped off the radar, announcing his hiatus from the field.[64] My attempts to contact him around 2012 all failed. At the time, I felt lucky answers to some questions could be culled from his 2007 *Lewiston Sun Journal* interview.[65] I was delighted when he popped back up in 2015. He remains active in the community.

I finally interviewed Chris via phone in February 2019. We talked about many things, including a personal encounter on November 11, 2007, in Enfield. You can hear recordings from that night on the first episode of Bob Coyne's podcast, *Bigfoot Quest*.[66] He hopes Maine investigators and eyewitnesses will cooperate with each other and create an environment where we are better able to help each other out.

Loren Coleman is founder and director of the International Cryptozoology Museum in Portland. The most visible of all Bigfoot investigators in Maine, Coleman ranks globally in the field of cryptozoology. Rather than write about him here, I would instead recommend you read some of his books, especially *Mysterious America* and *Bigfoot! The True Story of Apes in America*. He has been a good friend and staunch supporter of my work since we first met during a *Strange Maine* interview that I did with him at his home many years ago, not long after I started my blog.

IN RESEARCHING THIS BOOK, I attempted to share information with and interview people in the Maine Bigfoot field, with varying degrees of success. Some ignored my attempts or were simply nowhere to be found. Many were immediately helpful, and I am happy to call them my friends today.

A large number of them traced their interest in Bigfoot back to feature films like *Half-Human, Sasquatch: Legend of Bigfoot* and *Legend of Boggy Creek*, which they saw as youngsters. For some, this alone lit a lifelong fire of curiosity. As adults, they began to connect the dots between those films and local legends heard from coworkers and neighbors. They began looking at their Maine surroundings with new awareness.

Many have had personal encounters, and while they admit these brushes with the unknown were often "inconclusive," they were enough to keep them searching for better proof.

Few people these investigators come in contact with have heard of Bigfoot in Maine, though most are familiar with popular Pacific Northwest stories. Most Mainers they've talked to assume sightings are misidentifications of a bear or a hoax or simply delusions on the part of the witness. The exceptions are found near areas of repeated sightings, where some folks think nothing of the occurrences—it is a run-of-the-mill part of life for those in the know. When I asked Maine investigators what local Bigfoot accounts are key, Mount Katahdin legends and/or reports rank consistently high. On the national scene, the Patterson-Gimlin footage holds the star spot for them.

The investigators who engage in field research most often are those whose jobs facilitate this or those retired from regular employment. The others find themselves regularly stymied by their busy schedules. There are no idle rich investigators in Maine among those I encountered; they all have day jobs or are only recently retired from them.

When asked which areas of Maine are promising locations, most investigators pointed north of Bangor. The exceptions were the Leeds/Turner area, which is in southern Maine, and along the Maine–New Hampshire line between Fryeburg and Berwick. The Rangeley Lakes region merits future attention as well. They predict the swath of forested wilderness north of Bangor will become the real star of the show. It stands to good reason. Anyone or anything craving obscurity and scarcity of human contact would be happy to call that region home.

All of the investigators I interviewed prescribe to the no-kill philosophy, as do I.* However, they know the scientific community will not accept the existence of Bigfoot without (as biologist Merchant puts it) a holotype. With that in mind, while thorough visual documentation is essential, closure will not be achieved without trapping a Bigfoot to obtain biological samples straight from the source for DNA analysis. Michael Merchant remarks, "As valuable as eyewitness reports are, they only give us a starting point, and on their own, prove nothing. To establish proof for outlandish claims, we need outlandish proof."

They offer encouragement and guidance to those hoping to join the pursuit. Patience is a must. Awareness is essential. Certainly, don't go out in the field without learning basic wilderness survival skills. For instance, Merchant points out, "I carry pretty much the same gear in my pack for a day hike as for a long-term hike, since you never know when a day hike might become an overnight hike." Learn your local fauna and flora—it's the only way to recognize something out of the ordinary. Awareness of potential food sources in the area is another clue to locating animals. Keep your perspective so over time, you'll be able to spot patterns in the greater picture. Be skeptical, step carefully, record everything and, above all, be sure to enjoy your time out in the wild.

Are you good at snapping clear photos of wildlife when you encounter them? Can you get better? You are urged to do so by Michael Merchant and every other person I talked to. Merchant stated to me in 2012:

> *We are seeking a creature that is the most reclusive and elusive animal on the planet. It is an expert at avoiding humans. The only people who, in my opinion, have any chance of repeatedly encountering the creature will be those individuals who have taken the time to educate themselves to the point that they can go into an area and see, record and photograph every other animal that lives there. If you are out looking for Bigfoot and you can't get photos of deer, bear, moose, bobcats, fisher, mink, otters, etc., what chance would you have to encounter something much rarer, smarter and more elusive?*

When I asked these guys what the most essential field item to bring with them is, all of them came to one conclusion: a clear head and keen eye are vital. Your own brain is your best tool.

---

* For a comprehensive look at why we might need to reconsider this touchy subject, see Maine author Dan Drayer's book, *The Sasquatch Hunter's Field Manual: A Guide for Bringing the Creature into the Realm of Science* (2016), which is a straightforward and well-thought-out analysis of the practical points to be considered regarding this volatile but pertinent issue.

Chris Julian knows that sitting on a computer or reading books only gets an investigator so far. "I think people need to spend more time actually looking out in the woods." Real-life experience is where it's at. That's not to say that research isn't useful. A comprehensive scan of an area you're intending to hike using a good map system like Google satellite maps can save you some real headaches. The visible terrain can give you a better idea about what type of footwear to bring, and how much bushwhacking you'll be doing, and an aerial preview gives you a broad view of the area and useful landmarks before you visit it in person. And don't forget to check the weather forecast. Seriously, folks.

You will probably be surprised by what you find when you stick your head outside—Bigfoot or not. Julian is continually reminded that you don't need to look far in Maine—there is often something just past your own backyard. Michael Merchant reminds us that boots-on-the-ground immersion is vital to a chance at repeated success: "If you are unable to be comfortable deep in the forest, unable to survive in the deep woods where these creatures spend the majority of their time, your chance of success is low. I cannot express this enough. Too many people without wood skills mistakenly interpret signs of other animals for Sasquatch. The only way to know what you are doing is to get educated about the wilderness."

As this book goes to press, new people are already adding their voices to the established mix. In March 2020, the Maine Bigfoot Foundation[67] filed with the state of Maine to become an entity. I look forward to working with them.

25

ANIMAL PLANET'S *FINDING BIGFOOT* IN MAINE

W hen discussing awareness of Bigfoot in Maine after January 10, 2016, one must acknowledge the cultural landscape has changed. That evening, Animal Planet aired "Bigfoot's Maine Event." For those aware of Bigfoot activity in Maine, this was the moment it was no longer their secret. Now the entire *Finding Bigfoot* fanbase knew something squatchy was going on in our woods.

BFRO involvement in the Maine scene has varied over the years. According to Matt Moneymaker, a red herring Craigslist post fishing for Maine sightings in November 2013 was a hoax.* However, it planted a seed through press articles of the time,[68] triggering submissions of eyewitness reports and paving the way for *Finding Bigfoot* to visit.

This wasn't the first BFRO visit to our state. In May 2007, Matt Moneymaker stated, "We want to do an expedition in Maine next year."[69] From June 5 through June 8, 2008, BFRO member Nick Maione led a group to an undisclosed location chosen because of prior activity patterns.[70] While "the Maine expedition did not yield any definitive signs of a local [Bigfoot] population,"[71] it was not for lack of standard BFRO-style efforts. The area was subjected to a schedule of call blasting, pheromone baiting,

---

* Matt Moneymaker is one of the *Finding Bigfoot* team members, as well as the founder and president of the Bigfoot Research Organization (BFRO), the most high-profile Bigfoot investigation network in the United States.

wood-knocking and surveillance with game cameras and thermal imaging devices, mounted by small teams over a wide perimeter. Of the twelve or so attendees, plenty were from away.[*]

Five years later, in July 2012, a representative from *Finding Bigfoot* (Ping Pong Productions) emailed me, stating, "Animal Planet's 'Finding Bigfoot' is considering Maine for future episodes." But not until early 2015 did rumor became reality. The first step was a town hall–style meeting. In a February 2015 article,[72] eyewitnesses were invited to contact Loren Coleman with details of their encounters. Those who passed muster could attend the meeting, which was closed to the general public. I attended under the auspices of my collaborative work with Coleman and his International Cryptozoology Museum.

On Friday, April 17, 2015, at 7:00 p.m. at Flanagan Farm in Buxton, hubbub filled the hall. Attendees signed a nondisclosure agreement forbidding public discussion of the meeting until after air date. The stars of the show milled around, and excitement mounted until the team members—Matt Moneymaker, James "Bobo" Fay, Cliff Barackman and Ranae Holland—lined up at the front of the hall and brought the meeting to order.

The goal was to hear from Class A eyewitnesses about their encounters. Around twenty audience members out of about sixty total attendees stood up to speak that evening. Their encounters ranged from the late 1970s to a few months before the meeting. Tantalizing stories from neighbors and relatives were mentioned. Some accounts were dramatic, while others were more innocuous. I wanted to be able to relate them all to you, based on my notes taken during attendance, but unfortunately, the non-disclosure agreement I signed at the event precludes that occurring. We'll have to save that for a future date when I've interviewed all those eyewitnesses myself.

Local press coverage appeared only after the episode aired, much later.[†] The intervening months were rife with rumors, including speculation about cancellation of the series, but finally we had our chance to see the results, condensed into a digestible primetime serving. The upshot? The three-hour-long meeting boiled down to a few short minutes. The rest of the forty-nine-and-a-half-minute episode showed footage of the team visiting locations

---

[*] I was unable to tell from the message board posts if anyone was actually from Maine, but several attendees were identified in the discussion as having traveled to Maine from other states.

[†] Kathryn Skelton, "Weird, Wicked Weird: Maine Bigfoot Tales," *Lewiston Sun Journal*, January 17, 2016, https://www.sunjournal.com. Again, the nine-month delay was because everyone signed a nondisclosure agreement, agreeing not to divulge the details of the meeting publicly until after the episode aired.

with eyewitnesses and poking around in the Maine woods with their night vision gear, subjected to the wiles of our state's springtime weather. To their credit, they slogged through it gamely.

As of this writing, the episode is still available for viewing on the Animal Planet website: https://www.animalplanet.com/tv-shows/finding-bigfoot/full-episodes/bigfoots-maine-event.

26

ODDITIES AND HOAXES

A Mélange of Mysteries, Some Solved

Among every history of Bigfoot sightings are inevitably a few pranksters who cannot resist joining in and some folks obsessed in their own particular way.

Set in Stone?

One person with a longtime perplexing Bigfoot association is Tony Martin, who found some interesting relics in Coos Canyon in 1975. He found the foot-shaped rocks in a clay bed while exploring near the Swift River in Byron. As recently as a 2007 *Lewiston Sun Journal* article,[73] Martin was adamant that he had found a pair of fossilized Bigfoot tracks. According to the *Sun Journal* article, each stone is approximately five pounds and a foot long, and Martin mused about someday donating the specimens to the University of Maine at Farmington (UMF). I contacted the UMF Natural Sciences department to find out if the items had ever been donated but received no response.

Another interesting rock-bound pair of prints, commonly known as the Devil's Footprint, is located in North Manchester. While one of the footprints is more human or hoof-like, the other is large and gorilla-like, showing toes. The legend emerges from history, already misty by 1976, when an article appeared in the *Kennebec Journal*.[74] Lyle Strickland of Belgrade told reporter Wendy Hazard the tale:

About 100 years ago, a cantankerous road commissioner from Manchester was ordered by the town selectmen to fix the road….A large stone in the middle of the road had made it almost impassible for buggies and wagons.… The road commissioner…had worked up a furious temper and had let loose a stream of curses all afternoon. Finally at dusk, in the height of his fury, he told his men, "We'll give it one more try. God damn it and I swear to you if that rock would be moved, I would sell my soul to the devil."

The rock remained where it was as the oxen strained, and the chain slipped yet again. Disgusted, the commissioner dismissed the team for the day and went to bed for what turned out to be a very unwholesome sleep indeed. In the night, he roused his brother with his cries, feverish and in great pain. On hastening to fetch the doctor, the brother was astonished to see a large black dog lying on their doorstep. The dog ran into the house, where he hid under the commissioner's bed.

At his wits' end, the brother scrambled off to fetch the physician. On their return, the dog bolted out past the two men. The commissioner lay extinct on his bed, but the strangeness was not yet done. "The following day, the road crew returned to the Scribner Hill road.…To their amazement, they discovered a crater where the rock had lain the day before. The rock itself had been rolled off the road and placed beside the cemetery wall. In it was the large footprint (14 inches long and over 7 inches wide). The footprint they believe was the devil's own."

You can see the rock for yourself if you visit the North Manchester Meeting House at 144 Scribner Hill Road. The rock is at the corner of the wall beside the meetinghouse, which the footprints face.[75] The prints are worse for wear and don't show the detail in the toes that was visible in 1976. At some point, they were painted red to make them stand out, so it's easy to spot them.

Ways to Freak Out Hunters

Elsewhere in the Maine Bigfoot scene, there are traces of jokesters having fun with their friends, oftentimes visible in fleeting comments on Facebook, where knowing banter mentions the search for "whoever was wearing the gorilla suit." Sometimes it's someone who warns you that if anyone ever tries to tell you about the "Porter bog man," it was a story they made up and spread around as a kid.

Then of course there are the guys who have life-size plywood silhouette cutouts of Bigfoot propped up in their fields or by their garage, take your pick. I know of at least one of them near Waldoboro and have heard of several more. It's as calculated to make you jump in your driver's seat as the folks who do the same with life-size moose cutouts up in Aroostook. Yikes.

Some stories emerge from old newspapers, like the October 17, 1994 article where Bangor's Castle of Costumes store owner Marlene Paulette recounted a custom job for a local oil company executive. He thought it would be funny to "prowl the Maine woods dressed as a shaggy Sasquatch in order to frighten some colleagues gathered at a hunting camp."[76] He's lucky he didn't get shot.

Of course, there are also many stories posted online that never happened, and they just keep piling up. There is an entire blog[77] pretending to publish historic Bigfoot stories that are entirely made up, which has probably fooled a lot of folks who don't fact-check.

An article from 2018[78] recounted a story from retired Maine guide Dave Carey, based out of Rangeley. He went to great pains to convince a couple of out-of-state policemen that they were going to hunt a Bigfoot instead of the bear they hired him for. He cut a plywood footprint to leave tracks in mud by their bait site and mounted a sign on the nearby logging road, which mentioned a recent Bigfoot sighting, requesting hunters notify the University of Washington of any encounters. Then he convinced a local barber to give him hair clippings, which he placed strategically near the footprints. The clients were "freaked out" and even dialed the number on the sign.

And herein lies a clue to the hoaxer—he is willing to go to lengths that no one would believe reasonable, purely for the purpose of goosing his victims. Some do it undeniably for the attention and the entertainment value. For others, it is the adrenaline of the chase and the spook. But they all get creative when it's time to do the work, and the things they are willing do are flabbergasting. When a victim encounters the results, the furthest thing from their mind is that another person might be the source of their panic attack because who in their right mind would put all that work into something so ridiculous? The lazy armchair hoaxers are those who try to take credit for an encounter that they just read about in the paper and are the lamest of the bunch.

It's no wonder so many eyewitnesses are reluctant to come forward. The reasons include: what if no one believes me? What if everyone thinks I'm crazy? Or more relevant to this chapter, what if they think I'm stupid and fell for someone's prank? Maine's long history of tall tale tellers and jokesters offsets its tradition of taciturn citizens in a tense push-pull relationship. Bigfoot enthusiasts and researchers alike get worked up over the topic of hoaxes. Most Bigfoot chat boards clam up and become hostile as soon as they think they have a hoaxer on their hands, unwilling to chance giving information away that might improve the tools of those whose mission is to hoax the Bigfoot-loving public. Let me tell you, it can put a real damper on a previously interesting conversation.

But unfortunately, all of this just amuses the hoaxers even more, because serious Bigfooters really get their knickers in a twist over this stuff, and who could blame them? It creates huge obstacles to respectability and legitimacy in the field and causes long-lasting damage, which I have seen time and time again at all different levels, to individual lives and whole communities.

WHERE OH WHERE IS MY YARWEN?

Loren Coleman has run up against hoaxes over and over again. In 2006, he documented a peculiar chain of events set in motion by someone seeking exorbitant financial gain.[79] A person claimed they had a "Yarwen,"* describing a Bigfoot-like creature.

Their offer was promptly withdrawn when, Coleman states, "I wanted more details, plus a photograph, as well as to know the real identity of the person writing me." Coleman published the email, in which Dominick Perez claimed he "slew" an adult "yarwen" and kidnapped its cub, working all day on Friday September 1, 2006, "to bury the carcass of the adult so that no one could claim it. It was about 8.5 feet tall, with orange-brownish hair, and extremely heavy." He claimed the cub was 3.5 feet tall, weighing 121.5 pounds, adding, "It is extremely docile. I cannot tell what sex it is." The only other detail he willingly disclosed to Coleman was in response to his query about how he had transported it across multiple state lines: "To answer your last question, I drove the thing all the way home in the back of my truck handcuffed to the roll bar."

---

* Coleman surmised that while a Yarwen is a creature name used in fantasy gaming systems, perhaps the person meant Yeren, another name for a Bigfoot-type creature in Chinese lore. French hominologist Jean luc Drevillon speculated the person was a Star Wars fan, as there is an obscure Wookie character named Yarwin.

He was holding the cub at an undisclosed location. He wanted Coleman to travel to New Jersey to see it. His objective? Money. "I am aware of the million-dollar reward for the capture of one of these creatures, but that is not enough money for me," he stated. "I want to retain you as my representative, as I wish to remain anonymous. I want $100,000 for photos, which you can come and take….Together we can make history and get rich. I want you to list the creature on Ebay with an opening bid of $10,000,000. I will give you 10 percent of whatever we eventually get, and you will have the honor of breaking the story."

The entire ploy seemed ludicrous. As Coleman commented in his post, "When I hear about all the money someone thinks they deserve for their evidence, red flags go up for me." It was clear the person didn't know Coleman well at all, and they weren't interested in giving Coleman any assurances that would justify a long drive from Maine to New Jersey.

By the end of the negotiations (which were over within about twenty-four hours), the person became belligerent and told Coleman, "I'll tell you what…look on Ebay in about a week, and you will see a live video. I will give the exclusive story to one of your competitors….I will show nothing until I am paid for it." He signed off, saying curtly, "This ends my communications with you." The entire affair is disturbing.

What was the upshot? Well, Perez claimed he sold the creature for $17 million. Nothing else was ever heard about it. The public can draw its own conclusions from the sequence of events.

Using Bigfoot as Leverage

On August 11, 1993, the *Lewiston Sun Journal* published a story by reporter Jennifer Sullivan, detailing a sighting of "Big Foot" [*sic*] in Fryeburg.[80] In recent weeks, there had been a massive uptick in nuisance bear encounters in the area, but Fryeburg police chief David Miles was understandably surprised to meet a Portland TV news crew in his office inquiring about something else entirely.

"They arrived at my office telling this tale of this family on Route 113 that claimed to have seen Big Foot crossing the road," he recounted. "They got out of the car and took pictures and looked in the woods. They said they saw a footprint 15 to 18 inches in length." Chief Miles might have raised his eyebrows at the fact that they contacted a television station instead of local authorities. The family was identified as that of Brent Armstrong, from Wareham, Massachusetts, but as Armstrong did not have a listed phone number, the *Sun Journal* was unable to interview him before going to press.

Chief Miles remained unconvinced about Bigfoot's presence. The *Sun Journal* reporter resorted to speculating that the family had actually seen Elvis. Little did she know how close she was to the truth.

By August 14, the dream was over, albeit with a pretty darn weird ending.[81] "Attention Sasquatch fans and Yeti watchers: That hairy 7-foot creature who's been roaming the banks of the Saco River is a fraud." A thirty-year-old Gorham man "says he did it all for rock 'n' roll." That's right. Musician Martin Kade had "spent many a night since June 14th lying in bushes along roads in Fryeburg, Lovell, and Stow, trying to startle innocent passersby" with his homemade monster. He made the creature out of papier mâché and fake fur. For good measure, he also constructed twenty-two-inch-long monster feet to leave mysterious footprints.

Why, you might ask, was this fully grown male human spending his spare summer evenings gallivanting about in the shrubbery along the sideroads of Maine? Well, he thought it was a good way to get a recording contract. No, I'm not kidding, and neither was he. "'There's a lot more that you don't know,' an ominous Kade told the *Sun Journal* reporter."

The beginnings of his story will be familiar to many a Maine musician. Martin Kade and the Fictitious had been trying but failing to make it big. In April 1993, Kade decided "it was time for drastic measures." He didn't have money for a manager and record companies ignored them. But a silver lining gleamed when Kade heard that Maury Povich (I told you this was going to get weird) was visiting Maine for a charity golf tournament. If he could get the attention of this televisual tabloid-monger, he'd win a spot on his show because of the Bigfoot fiasco and then have a stage from which to sing to the world. At this point, I should mention Kade's appearance would be a solo one, as his bandmates had all quit, due to being "so humiliated by his tactics over the last few months." Kade's sole goal was to get his name into the news. He had even installed campaign signs throughout southern Maine that said, "Martin Kade for What?"

Kade focused his efforts on campers in the Saco River area. He would hide in the shrubbery, flat to the ground, and wiggle the monster about a bit before hiding it from view again. Sometimes for a change of pace, he'd try to give the suggestion that it was walking. Then he would saunter into the campsite an hour or so later. "I'd say, 'Hey, I heard you guys saw Big Foot [*sic*]. Did you report it?' They'd say, 'Yeah, I saw it, but people will think I'm crazy,' he recalled."

Once he put on a show for four women canoeing. Paddling within twenty feet of his lair, they still couldn't figure out what was going on. When he struck up a conversation with them later, per usual, he recalled, "They said they couldn't quite make out the whole thing, but they were sure it was dancing. One woman was all worked up about it." But still no Povich.

Another friend, trying to be helpful, talked to Portland television station WGME, claiming he'd seen the hairy beast on Route 113 in Fryeburg, and a film crew was sent out to cover the story again. Kade brought his monster to the Falmouth Country Club, carrying a sign with his phone number on it, lobbying Maury Povich to call him. He claimed to have called Povich in New York "a hundred times." Kade admitted to exhibiting exemplary restraint in not going after Povich whole hog while he was in Maine, since the celebrity was on vacation. If this was Kade's idea of taking it easy, I can't imagine him at full throttle.

Kade remained unrepentant. "'I'd do it all over again,' he said. 'There's going to be a lot more of this stuff from me. Probably not in Maine, though. I'll probably have to go somewhere where there's more of a music business so I can get noticed.'" It looks like he took that aim to extremes and left the country entirely, because he's been playing jazz and blues in the Stuttgart region of Germany for some years. I tried contacting him but did not hear back.*

---

* I contacted the reporter from the original articles, hoping she had additional insight into Kade's behavior or a better description of his puppet. She apologized for not remembering additional details about the story but was amused to read the articles again after all these years. She left the field of journalism after working in Maine dailies from 1979 to 1994 and did not keep her notes after shifting professions.

27

AN OVERVIEW AND SOME OPEN-ENDED CONCLUSIONS

When I started this book, I was interested in the topic but reserved judgment. I imagined I wouldn't find many astonishing stories, but with diligence, I could amass enough historical traces and anecdotal accounts that it would create a tapestry. With any luck, the fabric of all these accounts woven together would create patterns.

All these years later, I am surprised at the changes in my perspective. Talking to eyewitnesses and hiking on-site locations changed everything for me. My appreciation of Maine expanded to a much broader view.

I maintain my hypothesis that Maine is capable of feeding and sheltering a population of large mammals of this type. I further affirm that Maine allows ample concealment for a large mammal of this type. These ideas are supported by historic accounts, interviews and known environmental data.

What I have been able to conclude so far is that Mainers are encountering something out in the woods that does not match known large mammals in either appearance or behavior.

Certain parts of Maine have a history of activity that fits the pattern of behaviors attributed nationwide to Bigfoot-related incidents: structure building, trackways of footprints, objects being lobbed at human residents paired with vocalizations and noisy territorial protective behavior in the trees, chance sightings of creatures traveling or feeding, alone or in small family groups.

Some areas continue to experience, by all accounts, regular (if seasonal) activity along those same lines. There are clusters of sightings in areas that hint at a regular territory through which, like black bears, a small family group seems to roam, making use of the area's resources and shelter as the seasons change, with less activity in the winter months. Dense plant growth throughout the state fed by natural springs creates both food for foragers and sheltering undergrowth for travelers and lodgers.

Maine's heavily ridged landscape, formed so long ago by ancient glaciers passing by, creates an ideal terrain for maintaining invisibility. Ridges provide both vantage points during travel and quick barriers to disappear behind when needed. From the more rolling pockets in southern Maine to the steeper ridges at the central and western part of the state, the terrain provides ample cover.

The areas where sightings have piled up are many. In fact, as I realized when I tried to put together this summary, they sprawl all across the state, following its ever-present waterways and forests. It makes up not so much a map of individual hot spots as a network of activity based around the same natural Maine resources that we Mainers known and love ourselves.

The areas where clusters of eyewitness sightings occur in my research are:

- On the southwestern tip of Maine in York County and up the New Hampshire border
- In southern Maine along the Androscoggin River
- Sections of Somerset County
- In the mid-coast area leading out to Mount Desert Island
- In central Maine along the Penobscot and Kenduskeag Rivers
- On the northeastern edge of Maine along the Canadian border, leading up into the vast areas of Northern Maine and Aroostook County

Accounts of sightings continue to trickle in, many of them spanning the last dozen years or so, with new ones occurring all the time. A quiet neighborhood in West Baldwin is startled by a figure passing through yards and banging on sheds during the day while most of the neighbors are away at work. A trackway is found in the Wiscasset area. Something howls in Enfield.

As in any population, some neighbors get along better than others. Sometimes things don't work out and someone has to move elsewhere to get the peace and quiet and elbowroom they were looking for. But in general, respect for one another's privacy works out best for everyone concerned.

One never knows who one's neighbors are. *Illustration by Michelle Y. Souliere.*

As I've told many people, I feel like this book is only the beginning. I hope to hear about many more encounters in the coming years, and I look forward to the opportunity to hike into the Maine woods and learn more about our forests and everything that lives in them.

Here's to getting to know Maine even better.

NOTES

Part I

1. Maine Department of Inland Fisheries and Wildlife and Craig R. McLaughlin, "Black Bear Assessment and Strategic Plan, 1999," Resource Management Documents. https://digitalmaine.com/brm_docs/8, 7.
2. "Unorganized Territory," Wikipedia, https://en.wikipedia.org.
3. "List of States and Territories of the United States by Population Density," Wikipedia, https://en.wikipedia.org.
4. McLaughlin, 44.
5. "Black Bears," Maine Department of Inland Fisheries & Wildlife, https://www.maine.gov.
6. McLaughlin, 7.
7. Ros Coward, "Jane Goodall: New Mission for Chimps' Champion," Guardian, October 10, 2004, https://www.theguardian.com.
8. Dorothy Shaw Libbey, *Scarborough Becomes a Town* (Scarborough, ME: Bond Wheelwright Co, 1955), 166.
9. Josiah Pierce, *A History of the Town of Gorham, Maine* (Portland, ME: Foster and Cushing, 1862), 236–7.
10. Hosmer, *Historical Sketch*; as referenced by fellow Maine oddity enthusiast Dan Soucy in posts online and in his book Maine Monster Parade (Lulu, 2008).
11. John Langdon Sibley, *A History of the Town of Union, in the County of Lincoln, Maine: To the Middle of the Nineteenth Century* (Boston: B.B. Mussey and Co., 1851), 407.

12. Samuel Llewellyn Miller, *History of the Town of Waldoboro, Maine* (Waldoboro, ME: Heritage Books, 1910), 107

13. Joseph Griffen, ed., *History of the Press of Maine* (Brunswick, NJ: Press of J. Griffin, 1872), 193.

14. *Bangor Daily Whig and Courier*, August 11, 1846.

15. Dow, *Reminiscences of Neal Dow*, 35.

16. *Bar Harbor Record*, August 17, 1895; *Boston Daily Globe*, August 9, 1895.

17. "Terrible Wild Man in Maine," *Eau Clair (WI) Daily Free Press*, November 9, 1886. Courtesy of Chuck Flood.

18. Nok-Noi Ricker, "Bigfoot in Maine? 10-Foot-Tall 'Wild Man' Was Killed in 1886, Newspapers Reported," *Bangor Daily News*, October 27, 2013; includes clipping from "A New Kind of Game," *Industrial Journal of Bangor*, October 8, 1886, reprinted from the *Waterville Sentinel*.

19. "A Terror in the Woods," *San Francisco Call*, November 27, 1895. Courtesy of Chuck Flood.

20. "State News," *Bar Harbor Record*, December 4, 1895.

21. "Wild Man at Large in Minot: Several Women Have Seen Him Rush through the Brush along the Highways to Minot Corner," *Boston Daily Globe*, July 21, 1896.

22. "A Wild Man: Strange Experience of Councilman Stinchfield of Auburn, in the Woods," *Kennebec Journal*, August 5, 1896.

23. "Maine Melange: Wild Man in the Woods May Be Aaron Learned," *Bangor Daily Whig and Courier*, August 17, 1896.

24. "Wild Man? A Man Acts Queerly in the Woods about Witch Spring," *Bath Independent*, June 25, 1898.

25. "Witch Spring: A Bubbling Fountain Dear to the Hearts of the Youth of Bath," Bath Independent, August 6, 1887.

26. "Poland's Wild Man. The Town Hunting Him: He Carries a War Club Decorated with Flowers—He Appears to Be Vicious," *Lewiston Evening Journal*, July 22, 1905.

27. "Sparks from Maine Wires," *Daily Kennebec Journal*, July 25, 1905.

28. "Wild Man in Riggsville: Strange Stories of Presence of an Unknown Frequenter of Woods," *Bath Independent and Enterprise*, May 18, 1907.

29. "Looking Back: 100 Years Ago, 1913," *Sun Journal*, Encore Magazine, September 11, 2013.

30. "Androscoggin Pomona Meets with Durham Grange," *Lewiston Evening Journal*, October 2, 1913.

31. "The Meddybemps Howler, Washington County, Maine," Bigfoot Encounters, http://www.bigfootencounters.com.

Part II

32. Hilsmeyer, Bruce. "Hairy Man: My Life with Big Foot—A Maine Woman Remembers." Lincoln County Television, camera/editing by Dave Svens, September 19, 2017, lctv.org/hairy-man.

33. Hilsmeyer, "Hairy Man."

34. "Brown Bullhead," Species Information, Maine Department of Inland Fisheries & Wildlife, www.maine.gov.

35. Linda Godfrey, "Maine Woman's Childhood Life with Bigfoot," *Linda Godfrey: Author & Investigator of Strange Creatures* (blog), September 26, 2017, lindagodfrey.com.

36. Hilsmeyer, "Hairy Man.

37. Phyllis Austin, "Animal Park," *Maine Times*, September 17, 1976, found via the Maine News Index by Abraham Schechter (Portland Room, Portland Public Library). Photos by Tom Jones.

38. "'Monster' Tracks Found in Durham Area; Still Unknown What 'It' Is," *Lewiston Daily Sun*, July 28, 1973.

39. "Is It a Bear? Phantom? Or a Real Live Chimp?" *Maine Sunday Telegram*, July 29, 1973.

40. Seth Koenig, "Sasquatch Search Has Been Renewed in Durham, and 'Survivor' Bob Is on the Case," *Seth and the City* (blog), *Bangor Daily News*, February 06, 2014, http://sethkoenig.bangordailynews.com.

41. Sara Anne Donnelly, "Ghost Town," Down East, October 2016, https://downeast.com.

42. Ben Goodridge, "The Legend of the Durham Gorilla," *Portland Press Herald*, October 28, 2016, http://www.timesrecord.com.

43. Austin, "Animal Park."

44. Durham Maine Historical Society, "How many of you have memories of Merrill Zoo that was once located on Shiloh Road?" Facebook, March 20, 2018, https://www.facebook.com/durhammainehistoricalsociety/posts/2073781342835786.

45. "Is Something out There?" *Somerset Reporter*, June 23, 1977.

46. "Viewers Report 'Sasquatch' Seen," *Bangor Daily News*, weekend edition, June 18–19, 1977.

47. "Fires Plague State's Forests," *Press Herald*. Reprinted in the *Kennebec Journal*, May 30, 1977.

48. Gene Letourneau, "Sportsmen Say: Was It a Bear or Bigfoot?" *Kennebec Journal*, July 4, 1977.

49. Wendy Bumgardner, "How Far Can a Healthy Person Walk?" Very Well Fit, July 16, 2019 https://www.verywellfit.com.

50. Ed Parson, "Hiking: Myth Versus Reality of Sasquatch in Ossipee Range," Bigfoot Encounters, https://www. bigfootencounters.com. Compiled verbatim *Conway Daily Sun*, November 24, 2006.

51. Possibly Edward W. Cronin, "On the Trail of the Abominable Snowman," *Reader's Digest*, March 1976, 131–36. This article condensed the contents of Edward W. Cronin, "Yeti: The Abominable Snowman," *Atlantic Monthly*, November 1975, 47–53.

52. "Hudson, Maine: Historical Population," Wikipedia, last edited on February 18, 2018, en.wikipedia.org.

53. Mark LaFlamme, "Face Time: Michelle Souliere—one 'strange' lady," *Lewiston Sun Journal*, February 7, 2016, sunjournal.com.

54. Seth Koenig, "Portland Author Looking for Maine Bigfoot Sightings for New Book," *Seth and the City* (blog), *Bangor Daily News*, January 14, 2016. sethkoenig.bangordailynews.com.

55. "Point Lookout Maine," Point Lookout Resort and Conference Center, 2018, visitpointlookout.com.

56. "Ellsworth, Maine Sasquatch Sighting Zen~Yeti Bigfoot," SnowWalkerPrime, interview by Michael Merchant, October 30, 2014, video, 42:18, youtu.be/5HVHbCnytQc.

57. Estes, *Behavior Guide*, 374.

58. You can find Dan's Youtube channel at https://www.youtube.com/user/mainesloneranger.

Part III

59. *Maine Bushcrafter* (blog), http://themebushcrafter.blogspot.com.

60. D.L. Soucy, YouTube, https://www.youtube.com/user/mainesloneranger.

61. SnowWalkerPrime, YouTube, https://www.youtube.com/user/SnowWalkerPrime.

62. "Sasquatch: New England We are excited to announce our latest project," Facebook, https://www.facebook.com/bill.brock.1806/videos/10156617589901528. Note: The voiceover on the video is my own voice, from an interview Bill did with me at the beginning of June 2018.

63. Maine Bigfoot Research, https://groups.yahoo.com/neo/groups/MaineBigfootResearch/info. (Now mostly defunct.)

64. Kathryn Skelton, "Weird, in Review," *Lewiston Sun Journal*, http://www.sunjournal.com.

65. Kathryn Skelton, "Looking for Bigfoot," *Lewiston Sun Journal*, December 1, 2007, http://www.sunjournal.com.

66. "Premier Show," Bigfoot Quest, November 28, 2007, http://www.blogtalkradio.com.

67. Maine Bigfoot Foundation, Facebook private group, https://www.facebook.com/groups/1630576770498772.

68. J.R. Mitchell, "Finding Bigfoot Coming to Maine?" Q106.5, http://q1065.fm; *Culture Shock* (blog) *Bangor Daily News*, cultureshock.bangordailynews.com.

69. Kathryn Skelton, "Bigfoot & ME," *Lewiston Sun Journal*, May 5, 2007.

70. "Maine Expedition: June 5–8, 2008," BFRO, http://www.bfro.net.

71. "BFRO Public Discussion Forum," Wayback Machine, https://web.archive.org.

72. Kathryn Skelton, "Animal Planet's 'Finding Bigfoot' Coming to Maine," Lewiston Sun Journal, February 26, 2015.

73. Kathryn Skelton, "Bigfoot & ME," *Lewiston Sun Journal*, May 5, 2007.

74. Wendy Hazard, "Halloween: Local Legends to Pass the Time Spookily," *Kennebec Journal*, October 30, 1976.

75. J.W. Ocker, *The New England Grimpendium* (Woodstock, VT: Countryman Press, 2010), 243.

76. Tom Weber, "Costumes Scare Up Old, New Fantasies," *Bangor Daily News*, October 17, 1994.

77. "1987, Baxter State Park, Maine: Bigfoot Seen Running Backward," Today in Bigfoot History, August 4, 2017, https://bigfoothistory.wordpress.com.

78. Deirdre Fleming, "Strange and Quirky Hunting Stories from Registered Maine Guides," *Portland Press Herald*, November 18, 2018, centralmaine.com.

79. Loren Coleman, "Yarwen: Captured in Maine," Cryptomundo, http://www.cryptomundo.com.

80. Jennifer Sullivan, "Big Foot 'Sighted' in Fryeburg," *Lewiston Sun Journal*, August 11, 1993.

81. Jennifer Sullivan, "Big Foot 'Sightings' Turn Out to Be Hoax," *Lewiston Sun Journal*, August, 14, 1993.

BIBLIOGRAPHY AND ADDITIONAL READING

Arment, Chad. *The Historical Bigfoot: Early Reports of Wild Men, Hairy Giants, and Wandering Gorillas in North America*. Greenville, OH: Coachwhip Publications, 2006.

Citro, Joseph. *Passing Strange*. New York: Houghton Mifflin Harcourt, 1987.

Day, Holman F. *Up in Maine: Stories of Yankee Life Told in Verse*. Boston: Small, Maynard & Co, 1901.

Dow, Neal. *The Reminiscences of Neal Dow: Recollections of Eighty Years*. Portland, ME: Evening Express Publishing Company, 1898.

Drayer, Dan. *The Sasquatch Hunter's Field Manual: A Guide for Bringing the Creature into the Realm of Science*. Self-published, 2016.

Estes, Richard. *The Behavior Guide to African Mammals: Including Hoofed Mammals, Carnivores, Primates*. Berkeley: University of California Press, 1991.

Gould, John. *Maine Lingo: A Wicked-Good Guide to Yankee Vernacular*. Camden, ME: Down East Books, 2015.

Green, Daniel S. *Shadows in the Woods: A Chronicle of Bigfoot in Maine*. Greenville, OH: Coachwhip Publications, 2015.

Griffen, Joseph, ed. *History of the Press of Maine*. Brunswick, ME, Press of J. Griffin, 1872.

Harris, Louise. *A Comprehensive Bibliography of C.A. Stephens*. Providence, RI: C.A. Stephens Collection Brown University, 1965.

———. *The Star of the Youth's Companion: C.A. Stephens*. Providence, RI: C.A. Stephens Collection Brown University, 1969.

Hosmer, George L. *An Historical Sketch of the Town of Deer Isle, Maine, with Notices of Its Settlers and Early Inhabitants*. Boston: Stanley & Usher, 1886.

Libbey, Dorothy Shaw. *Scarborough Becomes a Town*. Portland, ME: Bond Wheelwright Company, 1955.

Maine Department of Inland Fisheries and Wildlife and Craig R. McLaughlin. "Black Bear Assessment and Strategic Plan, 1999." Resource Management Documents. https://digitalmaine.com/brm_docs/8.

Munn, Charles Clark. *The Hermit: A Story of the Wilderness*. New York: Grosset & Dunlap, 1903.

Pierce, Josiah. *A History of the Town of Gorham, Maine*. Portland, ME: Foster & Cushing and Bailey & Noyes, 1862.

Pierce, William Curtis. *1792–1866 as a Western Maine Lawyer Saw It*. Typescript held at Maine Historical Society, Portland, ME, 1976.

Pinkham, Steve. *Old Tales of the Maine Woods*. Boston: Merrimack Media, 2012.

Shapiro, Harry. *Peking Man*. New York: Simon and Schuster, 1975.

Stephens, C.A. *Camping Out*. Hurst & Company, undated (post 1867).

Taylor, Daniel C. *Yeti: The Ecology of a Myth*. New Delhi: Oxford University Press, 2017.

Whitney, Ronald G. *The World of C.A. Stephens*. N.p.: Waynor Publishing Co., 1976.

INDEX

ABOUT THE AUTHOR

Michelle Souliere is an author and artist who lives in Portland, Maine, where she graduated from the Maine College of Art. She owns the Green Hand Bookshop, where you can find her most of the time, working in the bookmines. She lives with her husband, Tristan Gallagher (*Rad Wraith*), and their two cats, Meep and Mr. Biscuits.

Her work (both written and drawn) is driven by curiosity and inspired by Maine history, the Maine landscape and how we respond to it.

Her work as editor of the *Strange Maine Gazette* and its companion blog gave rise to her first book, *Strange Maine: True Tales from the Pine Tree State*, published by The History Press in 2010. Since then, she has been working on *Bigfoot in Maine* whenever she can, traveling around the state and interviewing eyewitnesses for this book.

You can buy books from her at greenhandbookshop.com or follow her online on Instagram @greenhandbooks.

Visit us at
www.historypress.com
....